BLESSED BY GOD IN SATAN'S WORLD

HOW ALL THINGS ARE WORKING FOR YOUR GOOD

Edward D. Andrews

BLESSED BY GOD IN SATAN'S WORLD

How All Things Are Working for Your Good

Edward D. Andrews

Christian Publishing House
Cambridge, Ohio

Copyright © 2018 Edward D. Andrews

All rights reserved. Except for brief quotations in articles, other publications, book reviews, and blogs, no part of this book may be reproduced in any manner without prior written permission from the publishers. For information, write, support@christianpublishers.org

Unless otherwise stated, Scripture quotations are from Updated American Standard Version (UASV) Copyright © 2022 by Christian Publishing House

BLESSED BY GOD IN SATAN'S WORLD: How All Things Are Working for Your Good by Edward D. Andrews

ISBN-10: 1945757884

ISBN-13: 978-1945757884

Table of Contents

Book Description 11
Preface 13
Introduction 15
CHAPTER 1: Living in the Last Days: A Scriptural Overview 17
    The Prediction of Difficult Times 19
    Satan's World and Human Imperfection 22
    The Reality of Spiritual Warfare 25
CHAPTER 2: Understanding God's Way Out 29
    The Promise of 1 Corinthians 10:13 31
    God's Faithfulness in Providing an Escape 34
    Practical Steps for Finding God's Way Out 36
CHAPTER 3: The Nature of Doubt and How to Overcome It 40
    Identifying Sources of Doubt 42
    Scriptures for Combating Doubt 45
    The Role of Prayer in Overcoming Doubt 47
    The Weight of Doubt 47
    What is Doubt? 47
    Unveiling the Sources of Doubt 48
    The Role of Prayer in Overcoming Doubt 48
CHAPTER 4: What Is Faith and How to Examine Yours 50
    The Biblical Definition of Faith 53
    Self-examination: Are You in the Faith? 55
    Growing in Faith Through Difficult Times 58
CHAPTER 5: How All Things Work Together for Your Good 61
    The Truth in Romans 8:28 64
    Real-life Examples of Trials Turning to Triumphs 66

Trusting God's Sovereignty 69
CHAPTER 6: Drawing Closer to God Amidst Difficulties 72
The Principle of James 4:8 74
Spiritual Practices for Intimacy with God 77
The Rewards of Being Close to God 79
CHAPTER 7: Steadfastness in Faith: A Lifelong Journey. 82
Understanding the Call to Steadfastness 84
Building Resilience in Faith 87
The Impact of Steadfastness on Christian Walk 89
CHAPTER 8: Walking Wisely in a World Governed by Satan 93
The Exhortation of Colossians 4:5 95
Practical Wisdom for Daily Living 97
Living as Salt and Light in the World 100
CHAPTER 9: When Things Don't Make Sense: Trusting God's Plan 103
The Mystery of God's Will 105
Biblical Figures Who Trusted God Despite Not Understanding 107
Gaining Peace Through Trust 110
CHAPTER 10: Final Thoughts: Never Shrink Back, Keep Walking with God 113
A Recap of the Christian Journey in Satan's World 115
Tools for Staying the Course 118
The Hope and Promise of Eternal Life 121

Book Description

In a world marked by suffering, chaos, and uncertainty, it's easy to succumb to the pressures of doubt, fear, and disillusionment. Many wonder how God can allow us to go through hardships or why seemingly bad things happen to good people. These challenges can leave even the strongest in faith questioning the very fabric of their spiritual beliefs. If you've ever found yourself in this quandary, then "BLESSED BY GOD IN SATAN'S WORLD: How All Things Are Working for Your Good" offers a comprehensive, theologically rich answer to your deepest questions.

Navigating the corridors of life in Satan's world is no small feat. Yet, this book unveils the Biblical truth that God's grace is sufficient even in the toughest times. Beginning with a foundational understanding of our current epoch as the 'Last Days,' the book takes you through the complex maze of spiritual warfare, providing scriptural guidelines to safely get to the other side. Crucial to finding your way is understanding God's way out of trials, as assured by 1 Corinthians 10:13. This book breaks down the nature of God's promise, offering practical steps to recognizing and seizing the lifelines God provides in the middle of your storms.

Doubt is a formidable enemy to faith. Understand its roots and learn how to vanquish it through prayer and scriptural insights. On this journey, you'll also examine the essence of faith, subjecting your own beliefs to the scrutiny of the Word of God, learning how to grow it even amidst difficulties. Romans 8:28 posits that "All things work together for good to them that love God." This statement is dissected and illustrated with real-life examples to assure you that even when things seem bleak, God is still in control.

How close are you to God? Can you draw closer? What are the rewards of doing so? This book goes beyond shallow platitudes and dives deep into these questions, offering substantive scriptural principles for fostering a closer relationship with God. Your walk in faith is a lifelong journey requiring steadfastness. What does that mean, and how can you ensure you're on the right path? This book offers tools and biblical wisdom for nurturing steadfastness and resilience in your faith.

Living wisely in a world governed by Satan is like walking through a minefield. Find out what the Bible says about conducting yourself in a manner that both honors God and keeps you safe. Finally, when you find yourself in confusing circumstances, learn how to trust God's plan even when things don't make sense. Concluding with a hopeful outlook on the promise of eternal life, this book serves as a holistic manual for the believer striving to live a blessed life in a world governed by Satan. A life where all things, even the seemingly bad ones, are working for your good.

Preface

In our spiritual walk, we often find ourselves grappling with paradoxes. On one hand, we believe in a God of immense power and boundless love. On the other hand, we live in a world that often seems to contradict this picture, a world characterized by suffering, injustice, and confusion. This raises a multitude of questions: How do we make sense of our lives in such a world? How do we reconcile our faith in God with the reality of life in a world governed by Satan? Is it truly possible to live a life that is blessed by God amidst such complexities?

This book, "BLESSED BY GOD IN SATAN'S WORLD: How All Things Are Working for Your Good," aims to address these questions head-on, providing not just theoretical solutions but practical guidance grounded in the Scriptures. It's designed to be a resource for believers—whether new in the faith or seasoned veterans—navigating the tumultuous waters of life in a fallen world.

The journey begins with a detailed analysis of living in 'the Last Days,' a time characterized by escalated moral decline and spiritual warfare. Recognizing the signs of the times isn't merely for the sake of awareness; it equips us to engage more effectively in the spiritual battles that lie ahead.

In these pages, you'll find a Biblical road map for overcoming common challenges such as doubt, examining the depth and breadth of your faith, and understanding how God's promises fit into your daily life. The book isn't just an exposé on the difficulties of life; it's an action guide, providing practical steps for living victoriously.

Each chapter is an invitation to delve deeper into the Scriptures and fortify your faith, not merely to confront the problems you're facing today, but to equip you for challenges you may encounter tomorrow. It aims to strengthen your conviction that God is in control, even when life suggests otherwise.

I pray that as you turn each page, you'll find not only answers but also the encouragement to live a life truly blessed by God, even in Satan's world.

Edward D. Andrews

May your journey through this book lead you closer to Jehovah, strengthening your resolve to trust in His promises and live a life pleasing to Him, secure in the knowledge that all things are indeed working for your good.

Edward D. Andrews

Author of 220+ book and the Chief Translator of the Updated American Standard Version

Introduction

The world we live in today often feels like a maze filled with twists and turns, roadblocks and pitfalls. From news headlines that broadcast crises and tragedies to personal struggles that weigh heavy on our hearts, the challenges seem unending. Yet, here you are, holding this book—eager, I hope, to find a way to make sense of it all, and to understand how you can be blessed by God in such a tumultuous environment.

This book isn't meant to serve as a magic formula or a quick-fix guide to bypass all of life's difficulties. Instead, it's designed to provide you with the spiritual compass you need to navigate through them. It's an invitation to dig deep into the wisdom of the Scriptures, which remain our most reliable source of guidance, and to discover Jehovah's plans and purposes for your life.

While the Preface gave you an overview of what to expect, this Introduction aims to prepare you for the exploration ahead. This journey will require an open heart and a willing mind. It's a journey that will not only explore the challenges but also the opportunities that come with being a believer in a world governed by forces hostile to Jehovah God and His people.

Are you familiar with the concept of a refiner's fire? In the process of refining metals like gold or silver, the raw ore is subjected to intense heat. The purpose is to remove impurities and produce a material of much greater value. Similarly, this book aims to help refine your understanding and faith, using the heat of life's challenges as a catalyst for spiritual growth and enrichment.

Over the course of the following chapters, we'll tackle a variety of subjects that are crucial for every believer striving to live a godly life. From understanding the nature of our times and the reality of spiritual warfare to deepening your faith and trusting in God's sovereignty, each topic builds on the last, presenting a holistic view of Christian living in a world that's far from perfect.

As you dive into the chapters, you'll find real-life examples, concrete action steps, and most importantly, Scriptural references to guide your way. So, come prepared to engage, question, and reflect. This is more than a book; it's a spiritual toolkit designed to empower you to live a life blessed by God in Satan's world.

So, are you ready to begin? The journey starts now, and I am honored to walk this path with you, guided by the light of God's inerrant Word.

CHAPTER 1: Living in the Last Days: A Scriptural Overview

Introduction: The Last Days as a Period of Transition

The concept of the "Last Days" often conjures up images of apocalyptic events, catastrophic disasters, and general upheaval. But from a Scriptural perspective, the term has nuances that extend far beyond doom and gloom. In fact, the Last Days can be viewed as a transformative period—a time when God's purpose for mankind and the earth comes to its fullness. Understanding this timeframe is not only essential for grasping the grand sweep of God's plan but also for finding our place within that divine arrangement.

The Biblical Timeline and the Last Days

The Bible provides a chronological roadmap for the Last Days, from the arrival of Jesus Christ to the eventual renewal of heaven and earth. This timeline is not allegorical but should be understood in a literal, historical-grammatical manner. It can be divided into major phases, including:

1. **The First Coming of Christ:** This marks the inauguration of the "last days" (Hebrews 1:2), with Jesus offering the ultimate sacrifice for mankind's sin.

2. **The Church Age:** This is the period after Christ's ascension and before His Second Coming, which we are presently in. It is characterized by the preaching of the gospel to all nations (Matthew 28:19-20).

3. **The Tribulation:** A seven-year period of extreme difficulty, culminating in the return of Jesus (Revelation 7:14).

4. **The Second Coming and Millennium:** Christ returns to establish a thousand-year reign on earth, fulfilling promises made to Israel and all believers (Revelation 20:1-6).

5. **The New Heaven and New Earth:** The ultimate renewal of all things (Revelation 21:1).

The Signs of the Times

Jesus, along with other Biblical writers, gives us several indicators to watch for, which signify that we are indeed living in the Last Days. These include but are not limited to:

- **Increased Knowledge and Technology:** Daniel 12:4 points out that knowledge will increase, and indeed, we've seen an exponential growth in technology and information in recent times.

- **Apostasy and False Teachings:** Scriptures like 1 Timothy 4:1 and 2 Timothy 4:3 warn of times when people will depart from the faith and give heed to doctrines of demons.

- **Global Upheavals:** Earthquakes, famines, and wars are described as the "beginning of sorrows" in Matthew 24:7-8.

Suffering and Persecution

Living in the Last Days does not exempt believers from trials. On the contrary, suffering and persecution are often intensified. Scriptures such as 2 Timothy 3:1-5 describe these times as perilous. However, rather than a sign of God's abandonment, suffering is permitted by God for reasons that serve His purpose. It tests faith, builds character, and ultimately works for the good of those who love Him (Romans 8:28).

God's Sovereignty in the Last Days

The overarching truth that believers must hold onto is the sovereignty of God. Despite the corruption of the world, God's purpose will be fulfilled. Revelation culminates with the picture of a New Heaven and a New Earth, where God will dwell with His people, wiping away every tear (Revelation 21:3-4).

The Role of the Believer

As believers in this age, we have unique roles to play. Unlike the idea of Calvinistic predestination, where one's fate is sealed regardless of choices, the Bible promotes active faith. Evangelism, staying true to sound doctrine, and living a godly life are critical tasks given to us. We are not souls trapped in bodies but are souls ourselves, striving to live in obedience to God's Word, guided not by an indwelling Spirit but by the wisdom contained in Scripture.

Blessed in the Midst of Trials

So, are we living in the Last Days? According to Scriptural evidence, it would seem so. Yet, this is not a cause for despair but for hopeful anticipation. For those who remain faithful, these times are not a countdown to destruction but a march toward ultimate restoration. By understanding the biblical narrative concerning the Last Days, we can better appreciate how all things, even those that seem adverse, are working for our good.

In the next chapters, we will delve further into each of these aspects, providing concrete examples, analogies, and explanations to equip believers for the unique challenges and unparalleled opportunities that come with living in the Last Days.

The Prediction of Difficult Times

Grappling with Challenges in the Last Days

The Last Days are often equated with difficult times—periods of suffering, trials, and moral decline. Understanding the scope and nature of these difficulties is not only instrumental for theological reasons but also vital for every believer's spiritual growth and endurance. The Bible is remarkably forthcoming about the hardships that will characterize this pivotal era. This chapter aims to delve into these Scriptural predictions and offer insights into how believers can navigate these turbulent times.

The Scriptural Forecast of Difficult Times

The apostle Paul, in his letters to Timothy, sketches an alarming but realistic picture of the Last Days. "But understand this, that in the last days difficult times will come," he writes (2 Timothy 3:1). The Greek word translated "difficult" is *chalepos*, which conveys the idea of harsh, fierce, or hard to bear circumstances. This description extends to various areas of life:

- **Moral Decay:** "For people will be lovers of themselves, lovers of money, boastful, arrogant, blasphemers, disobedient to parents, ungrateful, unholy" (2 Timothy 3:2).

- **Relational Strains:** Paul further states that people will be "unloving, irreconcilable, slanderers, without self-control, brutal, not lovers of good" (2 Timothy 3:3).

- **Religious Deception:** "Having an appearance of Godliness, but denying its power" (2 Timothy 3:5).

Such predictions echo throughout the New Testament, pointing to a collective moral and spiritual crisis.

The Underlying Causes of Difficult Times

Scripture is not silent about the root causes of these hardships.

1. **Human Depravity:** The sinful nature of humanity is a core reason for the degradation we witness. Paul highlights this in Romans 1:18-32, describing how mankind's rejection of God leads to all forms of ungodliness.

2. **Satanic Influence:** The apostle John describes the whole world as lying in the power of the wicked one (1 John 5:19). The enemy's schemes exacerbate the natural inclination toward sin.

3. **Apostasy:** 1 Timothy 4:1 warns that in latter times some will depart from the faith, paying attention to deceitful spirits and teachings of demons.

Understanding these causes helps in formulating strategies to counter them.

Navigating Personal Suffering

Many might wonder why God, being all-powerful, would permit such difficulties, even for His followers. While God is not the author of suffering, He allows it for purposes that ultimately conform to His will. Job's life is a classic example; his suffering tested his faith, refined his character, and brought him into a deeper relationship with Jehovah. The hardships of life act as a refining fire, purging impurities and solidifying our faith.

The Call to Vigilance and Endurance

The predicted difficulties should awaken a sense of urgency and vigilance among believers. Peter reminds us to be "sober-minded" and "watchful" because the devil prowls around like a roaring lion, seeking someone to devour (1 Peter 5:8). Vigilance does not imply a passive waiting but an active engagement with our faith. The book of Hebrews, commonly attributed to Paul, calls for "running with endurance the race that is set before us" (Hebrews 12:1).

The Role of the Church and Scripture

During difficult times, the Church and Scripture serve as God-given tools for perseverance. The Church acts as a spiritual haven, offering fellowship and accountability, while the Scriptures guide us in the paths of righteousness. We are not indwelt by the Holy Spirit; rather, we are directed by the wisdom contained in God's Word. Hence, the Bible serves as our primary source of instruction and inspiration, as stated in 2 Timothy 3:16-17, "All Scripture is inspired by God and beneficial for teaching, for rebuke, for correction, for training in righteousness; so that the man of God may be fully competent, equipped for every good work."

Remaining Blessed Amidst Difficulties

The fact that we are living in difficult times should neither surprise us nor dishearten us. These are prophesied aspects of the Last Days that serve both as warnings and as signs of the times. The key to navigating these challenges lies not in escapism but in understanding God's sovereignty and man's responsibility. The apostle James rightly encourages believers to count it all joy when facing trials of various kinds (James 1:2-4). These trials have a developmental function; they are tools in the hands of God, shaping us for the life to come.

In subsequent chapters, we will delve deeper into the biblical teachings that equip us to face these difficulties, always remembering that no matter how harsh the conditions, all things are indeed working for our good, in accordance with God's perfect plan.

By grasping the Scriptural predictions and injunctions regarding the Last Days, we prepare ourselves to live not as victims but as victors—blessed by God even in Satan's world.

Satan's World and Human Imperfection

The Inescapable Reality of Satan's Influence and Human Weakness

Navigating life in a world under the influence of Satan, while grappling with human imperfection, is a formidable challenge. Many believers struggle to reconcile the presence of evil with the omnipotence and goodness of God. This chapter aims to shed light on these complex issues, drawing upon the richness of biblical truth to offer not just understanding, but also guidance on how to remain steadfast in one's faith.

Satan's Dominion: The World in the Grip of the Evil One

Scripture is unequivocal: Satan has a level of authority over the world. In 1 John 5:19, it is said, "We know that we are from God, and the whole world lies in the power of the evil one." This does not negate God's ultimate sovereignty but speaks to the current condition of worldly systems and structures. *Why does God allow this?* It's essential to understand that God's allowance is temporary and serves a greater purpose in His redemptive plan. Satan's rule is permitted but not endorsed by Jehovah, who maintains ultimate control.

The Interplay Between Human Imperfection and Satanic Influence

Satan capitalizes on human frailties to extend his influence. The biblical account of Adam and Eve serves as an archetypal illustration. Their act of disobedience not only brought sin into the world but also illustrated how Satan exploits human weaknesses—like pride and desire—for his ends. However, their sin also marked humanity with imperfection, a reality we've inherited and must contend with.

Understanding the Nature of Human Imperfection

Human imperfection is not a mere character flaw but a deeply entrenched condition that affects our thoughts, desires, and actions. Paul provides a vivid portrayal of this in Romans 7:14-25, where he speaks of his struggle to do good in the face of indwelling sin. This imperfection is all-encompassing, a malaise that corrupts every part of our being.

The Triple Threat: The World, The Flesh, and The Devil

Christians often find themselves contending with not just one but three formidable enemies: the world, the flesh, and the devil. These forces operate synergistically to challenge a believer's spiritual well-being.

1. **The World:** A system opposed to God, characterized by materialism, secularism, and moral relativism.
2. **The Flesh:** Our human nature, inclined towards self-gratification and rebellion against God.
3. **The Devil:** The spiritual adversary who masterminds schemes to lead humanity away from Jehovah.

This triad forms a complex web of temptations and snares, requiring both wisdom and spiritual fortitude to navigate successfully.

Overcoming Through Biblical Wisdom and God's Providence

The Bible is the ultimate resource for understanding and overcoming both satanic influence and human imperfection. It doesn't promise us a sinless state in this life but equips us for the battle. Paul advises believers to "put on the full armor of God" (Ephesians 6:11) so that they can stand against the schemes of the devil. This involves both defensive and offensive strategies, grounded in truth, righteousness, peace, faith, and the Word of God.

Moreover, God's providence—His divine guidance and care—is an anchor for the believer. The promise of Romans 8:28 stands as a testament to God's control over all situations for the ultimate good of those who love Him. While we may not see the full picture now, we can trust that Jehovah is orchestrating events in line with His will, even when Satan seems to hold sway.

The Role of Prayer and Community

In battling the triad of the world, the flesh, and the devil, the importance of prayer and a strong Christian community cannot be overemphasized. These are not just religious activities but life-sustaining practices that empower believers to withstand trials. James 5:16 encourages believers to pray for each other, stating that "the fervent prayer of a righteous person is very powerful." It serves as a communication line with God and a fortification against satanic influence.

Finding Blessings Amid the Struggles

Living in Satan's world with human imperfection is undeniably difficult but not hopeless. The Bible offers the wisdom and the tools to not only navigate these choppy waters but also to find blessings amid the struggles. Jehovah has not left us to flounder in a world dominated by Satan; He has provided us with the means to live victoriously. Although we face the daily challenges of living in a fallen world, the promises of God and the hope of eternal life provide us with an anchor and a future.

The struggle against Satan's world and human imperfection will continue until God's redemptive plan reaches its climax. Until then, we find our strength in the promises of Scripture, the fellowship of believers, and the steadfast character of Jehovah God.

As we move forward in this book, we will delve deeper into the rich biblical teachings that not only help us understand our challenges but also guide us in overcoming them. We are not victims; we are more than conquerors through Him who loved us (Romans 8:37). By aligning ourselves with Jehovah and His Word, we can live blessed lives, even in Satan's world.

The Reality of Spiritual Warfare

Acknowledging the Unseen Battle

Spiritual warfare is a real, palpable reality that exists alongside the physical world. As believers in Christ, we are drafted into a cosmic conflict that started long before humanity's creation and will culminate only when God's redemptive plan is fully realized. Ignorance of this warfare leaves us vulnerable to spiritual casualties. This chapter aims to unveil the reality and nature of spiritual warfare, its manifestations, and the biblical solutions available for believers.

Edward D. Andrews

The Origins of Spiritual Warfare: A Cosmic Rebellion

Spiritual warfare did not begin with mankind; it began in heaven. Revelation 12:7–9 describes a celestial rebellion led by Satan against Jehovah. Expelled from heaven, Satan focused his malice on earth, plunging humanity into this cosmic struggle through the deception of Adam and Eve. The Bible declares, *"Be sober-minded; be watchful. Your adversary the devil prowls around like a roaring lion, seeking someone to devour"* (1 Peter 5:8). It's not folklore or symbolism; it's a cosmic reality that demands our attention.

The Battlegrounds of Spiritual Warfare

Spiritual warfare manifests in various aspects of life. While it's a cosmic conflict involving angelic beings, its battles are often fought in the recesses of human hearts, the dynamics of communities, and the broad societal structures that govern us.

The Individual Soul

Firstly, the individual soul is a primary battleground. Satan attempts to produce doubt, disbelief, moral corruption, and ultimately spiritual death. Our hearts and minds are the arenas where decisions are made either to yield to temptation or to follow the ways of Jehovah.

Within the Church Community

Another frontline is the church community. Satan infiltrates Christian fellowships to cause division, heresy, and spiritual lethargy. Paul warns against false apostles who are *"deceitful workmen, disguising themselves as apostles of Christ"* (2 Corinthians 11:13). Satan's schemes are often subtle and couched in the language of spirituality to confuse believers.

The Cultural and Societal Front

Finally, spiritual warfare extends to cultural and societal norms that are antithetical to godly living. From policies that oppose religious freedoms to entertainment that mocks Christian values, the social systems can be orchestrated by demonic influences to marginalize God's truth.

The Weapons of Our Warfare: Not Carnal but Mighty

Recognizing spiritual warfare is not enough; we must know how to fight. Paul mentions that *"the weapons of our warfare are not of the flesh but have divine power to destroy strongholds"* (2 Corinthians 10:4).

The Sword of the Spirit

One of the most potent weapons at our disposal is the Bible, referred to as the *Sword of the Spirit* in Ephesians 6:17. The Bible equips us with wisdom and fortifies our minds against deceptions. Jesus himself modeled this when he combated Satan's temptations by quoting Scripture (Matthew 4:1-11).

Prayer as a Weapon

Prayer is not merely a devotional exercise but a mighty weapon in spiritual warfare. In prayer, we align our will with God's, draw upon His strength, and invite His intervention in our battles.

The Shield of Faith

Faith is our protective shield. It's not a blind leap into the dark but a confident assurance in the character and promises of God, which equips us to fend off the fiery darts of the evil one.

Our Divine Commander and His Sovereignty

Jehovah is not a passive observer in this cosmic conflict. He is our Commander, actively leading us to victory. In His sovereignty, God has allowed the existence of evil for a time, but His ultimate victory is assured. Revelations 20:10 confirms that Satan will be thrown into the lake of fire, ending his reign of terror.

Practicing Discernment: Identifying the Enemy's Schemes

Discernment is a crucial skill in spiritual warfare. This isn't a mystical sixth sense but a practical ability developed through engagement with Scripture and a life of prayer. Discernment allows us to see behind the masks of situations and people to identify spiritual realities influencing them.

Conclusion: Triumph Through Obedience and Faith

We are not helpless in spiritual warfare; we are more than conquerors through Christ. Through obedience to God's Word and reliance on His grace, we can defeat the enemy's schemes. We are not fighting for victory; we are fighting from a position of victory, achieved by Christ on the cross.

As we navigate the challenges of life in these last days, let us not forget the invisible war raging around us. But let's also not forget the invincible God we serve, whose eternal plan encompasses not just the end of evil but the glorification of His children. We are not alone; our Commander is with us, and His victory is our inheritance.

By understanding the stakes, the battlefields, and the weapons available to us in this spiritual war, we can live a life of triumph, even in a world that stands under the sway of the evil one. The reality of spiritual warfare should neither paralyze us with fear nor inspire a morbid fascination, but drive us to greater dependence on Jehovah, who assures us the ultimate victory.

CHAPTER 2: Understanding God's Way Out

The Challenge of Life in a Fallen World

Life on earth can often feel like navigating a maze. Trials, temptations, and setbacks make us wonder, "Why is this happening to me?" We might even question the love and goodness of God during trying times. The first thing to understand is that living in a fallen world means facing challenges, but these challenges are not indicative of God's disfavor. Rather, they are the natural outcomes of a world that turned its back on its Creator. However, even in this bleak setting, God has provided a way out for each of us.

God's Sovereignty and Human Free Will: A Balanced Perspective

God is omnipotent, meaning He possesses infinite power. He is also omniscient, which means He knows all things, including future events and all the potential outcomes of free will decisions. However, it's crucial to clarify that God's foreknowledge doesn't negate human free will. We still have the ability to choose, and God respects that ability.

Imagine a parent who knows his child so well that he can predict the child's choices. Does the parent's understanding negate the child's freedom to choose? No, it doesn't. Similarly, God's foreknowledge does not "fix" our destiny; it simply means He knows what we are going to choose. This balanced view upholds God's sovereignty while recognizing human free will.

God's Object Lesson: The Role of Suffering

Suffering is a complex issue that often leaves us scratching our heads. Contrary to some beliefs, God didn't design suffering to foster growth, endurance, or character. However, He does allow it. Think of it as an object lesson to teach humanity about the consequences of sin and the importance of His sovereignty.

Picture a classroom where a teacher demonstrates the law of gravity by dropping an apple. The teacher doesn't cause gravity; he merely showcases its effects. Similarly, God allows suffering to reveal the natural outcome of sin and human independence from Him.

God's Way Out: Jesus Christ

"For God so loved the world, that he gave his only Son, that whoever believes in him should not perish but have eternal life." (John 3:16)

The provision God made for us is Jesus Christ, the ultimate solution to the problems and challenges we face. God's love compelled Him to offer His own Son as a sacrifice to atone for human sin. The death and resurrection of Jesus Christ provide us with a way to escape the eternal consequences of our wrongdoings. This isn't universal salvation where everyone is saved regardless of their beliefs or actions. Salvation is a gift, but like any gift, it must be accepted. Thus, it's crucial to recognize that Jesus is God's way out for us.

The Bible as Our Guide: No Indwelling of the Holy Spirit

While some believe in the indwelling of the Holy Spirit as a personal guide, it's important to note that the Bible itself serves as our guide. The Holy Spirit inspired the Word of God, but it doesn't reside in us.

Consider GPS technology. A GPS system doesn't need to be inside your car to guide you. It operates from a distance yet is immensely effective. Similarly, the Bible provides us with the directions we need to navigate life's complexities.

Obedience and Consequence: The Biblical Framework

One might ask, "If God provides a way out, why do some seem to suffer more than others?" The answer partly lies in the principle of obedience and consequence. While salvation is by faith, obedience to God's Word brings blessings, and disobedience leads to negative consequences.

For instance, consider the laws of physics. If you ignore the law of gravity and step off a cliff, you will fall. Similarly, ignoring God's instructions comes with its own set of consequences. However, these consequences are not divine punishments but natural outcomes.

Taking Hold of God's Provided Way

In a fallen world, challenges are inevitable. But God, in His infinite wisdom and love, has provided a way out through Jesus Christ. Our role is to accept this gift and live according to His Word. The challenges we face may not disappear overnight, but we can navigate them with a newfound hope and a clear path. Remember, the journey of faith is like walking on a well-lit path in the dark. Though you may not see everything clearly, the light from the Bible ensures you won't stumble.

God has not abandoned us in our trials and tribulations. He has provided a way out, and it's our responsibility to take hold of it. May you find peace and guidance as you walk in God's provisions, understanding that all things are indeed working for your good.

The Promise of 1 Corinthians 10:13

The Significance of 1 Corinthians 10:13

Let's begin by examining the verse in question. 1 Corinthians 10:13 reads: "No temptation has overtaken you that is not common to man. God is faithful, and he will not let you be tempted beyond your ability, but with the temptation, he will also provide the way of escape, that you may be able to endure it." This singular verse is a treasure trove of reassurance, guidance, and divine promise, highlighting God's active role in our lives as we navigate the challenges that inevitably come our way.

A Common Experience: Human Temptation

Firstly, it is vital to note that temptation is a shared human experience. The Apostle Paul reminds us that we are not alone in our struggle. Imagine you're part of a crew sailing through a storm. It's reassuring to know that other ships are sailing through the same turbulent waters. This collective human experience can give us strength. Knowing that others have faced similar situations—and have overcome—can be a source of motivation.

The Faithfulness of God

One of the most striking aspects of this verse is its declaration that "God is faithful." In a world that often feels unstable and unpredictable, these three words act as a pillar of stability. Imagine your life as a building. A building's stability depends on the foundation it's built on. If God's faithfulness is that foundation, then despite the storms that come, the structure—that is, your life—stands firm.

Limitations on Temptation

Paul tells us that God will not let us be "tempted beyond [our] ability." This part of the promise is akin to a safety net. In circus acts, high-wire performers have a safety net below. They may wobble; they may even fall. But the safety net is there to catch them. God, in His wisdom, knows our breaking point. He knows the point where temptation would be too much for us to handle, and He promises never to allow us to reach that point.

God's Escape Route

It's fascinating that God doesn't merely limit the level of temptation we'll face; He "will also provide the way of escape." Imagine being in a maze with various paths, some leading to dead ends and others leading out. God, in His providence, highlights the path of escape. However, it is essential to remember that having an "escape" doesn't mean the absence of difficulty. The way out is there, but we must be willing to take it. It's like a fire exit in a building. Knowing there is an exit doesn't automatically transport you outside; you must walk through it.

Endurance Over Escape

Lastly, the verse explains that God provides a way out so that "you may be able to endure it." The focus here is not merely on escape but on endurance. It's not just about getting out of a tough situation but coming out of it stronger. Picture a blacksmith working metal. The metal must endure the heat to be shaped into something new. Similarly, God allows temptations not to break us but to build character and resilience in us.

Balancing Sovereignty and Free Will

It is crucial to grasp that while God provides a way out, we have the free will to choose whether to take that path. God's foreknowledge doesn't restrict our choices. He knows all possible outcomes of our decisions, but the choice remains ours. It's like a chess master who, knowing all possible moves, can still be surprised by an opponent's choice.

Closing Thoughts

1 Corinthians 10:13 offers a balanced perspective on life's challenges and God's role in helping us overcome them. It is a promise rooted in God's character. A faithful God, fully aware of our limitations, not only restricts the trials that come our way but also actively provides an escape route. This promise, however, is not a

magic wand that makes difficulties disappear. It requires action on our part: the exercise of our free will to choose God's way, to endure, and to emerge stronger. So, when faced with life's inevitable difficulties, let's remember God's promise and take comfort in His faithfulness.

God's Faithfulness in Providing an Escape

The Immutable Nature of God's Faithfulness

Let's begin with a simple but profound truth: God is unchanging in His faithfulness. Think of it like the North Star—always in the same place, guiding travelers for centuries. No matter how dark our world becomes due to the consequences of sin and Satan's influence, Jehovah's faithfulness remains a constant source of guidance and hope for us.

"Know therefore that Jehovah thy God, he is God, the faithful God, who keepeth covenant and lovingkindness with them that love him and keep his commandments to a thousand generations," (Deuteronomy 7:9).

How Does God Provide a Way Out?

Imagine you're in a maze with walls too high to climb. Dead ends, winding paths, and it seems there's no way out. Then you find a map right in the middle of it all. It's as if someone knew you'd get lost and provided you with a way to navigate through the maze successfully. That's what God's Word does for us. It offers a roadmap to navigate the complexities of life in a world under Satan's influence. God does not keep us insulated from trials, but He always provides an escape—through His wisdom, through fellow believers, and most importantly, through Jesus Christ.

"There hath no temptation taken you but such as man can bear: but God is faithful, who will not suffer you to be tempted above that ye are able; but will with the temptation make also the way of escape, that ye may be able to endure it," (1 Corinthians 10:13).

The Role of Jesus Christ in Our Escape

No discussion about God's provision would be complete without focusing on Jesus Christ. God provided His Son as the ultimate "way out" of the bondage of sin and death. Jesus Christ is akin to a bridge that allows us to cross a chasm that we could never traverse on our own.

"For the wages of sin is death, but the free gift of God is eternal life in Christ Jesus our Lord," (Romans 6:23).

The Spirit-Inspired Word of God as Our Guide

While some may think of the Holy Spirit as a magical force that swoops in to pull us out of difficulties, the Bible presents a different view. We do not have the indwelling of the Holy Spirit. Rather, the Spirit has given us something incredibly powerful—the inspired Word of God. It's like a manual for a complex machine; it tells you how everything works and how to keep things running smoothly. Neglect it, and you're sure to have problems. Embrace it, and you find that it has answers to problems you didn't even know you had.

Living in a World of Suffering

We must also remember that God allows suffering to exist. This is not to say that He takes delight in our pain. Rather, God permits suffering to demonstrate the disastrous results of sin and rebellion against His sovereignty. Imagine a teacher allowing a student to make mistakes on a test. Those errors, while painful at the moment, serve as a powerful lesson for the future. In a similar way, the trials and tribulations we face are part of a broader object lesson in the consequences of straying from God's guidance.

What About Fate or Destiny?

It's common for people to think that some form of fate or destiny controls their lives, like a script that's already been written. But that idea runs contrary to the biblical view. God has not fixed our destiny;

we freely choose our path. Just as a skilled chess player knows all the potential moves on the board, God's foreknowledge encompasses all the choices we might make. However, He doesn't manipulate or control our decisions; He respects our free will.

A Personal Relationship with Jehovah

God's faithfulness extends to all humanity, not just a chosen ethnic group or a select few. While Jehovah had a covenant relationship with Israel, due to their disobedience and apostasy, they lost their special status. Thus, today, God's covenant relationship is open to everyone through faith in Jesus Christ. It's like being given a VIP pass that's valid for anyone who accepts it, not just a select group of people.

"For there is no distinction between Jew and Greek; for the same Lord is Lord of all, bestowing his riches on all who call on him," (Romans 10:12).

Living in a world influenced by Satan is undeniably challenging. Yet Jehovah, in His infinite wisdom and love, has made provisions for us to not only endure but also to thrive. Through His immutable faithfulness, the redemptive work of Jesus Christ, and the wisdom imparted in His Spirit-inspired Word, God has provided us a robust escape plan from the snares of life's difficulties. So as we navigate the labyrinth of life, let us cling tightly to these divine provisions, confident that with Jehovah's guidance, all things will indeed work for our good.

Practical Steps for Finding God's Way Out

The Landscape of Suffering and God's Sovereignty

We live in a world marred by sin, rife with suffering and hardships. Yet, God allows this reality for a purpose: not to foster growth or endurance, but as an object lesson for humanity. We have been living through a stark lesson that demonstrates the inherent flaw in human independence from God's sovereignty. Though suffering wasn't designed by God, its presence in our lives should serve as a constant reminder of our need for divine guidance.

The Necessity of Prayer: The First Step in Finding God's Way Out

When we find ourselves trapped in the maze of life's difficulties, the first step in finding God's way out is prayer. Prayer isn't merely a ritual or a set of memorized words. It is a heartfelt conversation with God, a way to draw close to Him and seek His guidance. *"Pray without ceasing,"* says 1 Thessalonians 5:17. Continuous, unceasing prayer keeps us connected to God, helping us discern His way out even in complex situations. A humble, sincere prayer is like a direct line to the heavenly Father, providing us not only with emotional relief but also spiritual clarity.

The Role of the Bible: God's Inspired Word as Your Guide

The Bible isn't just a book; it's the inspired Word of God, penned by men under the direction of the Holy Spirit. It serves as a lamp unto our feet, guiding us through the complex terrains of life. While we don't experience the indwelling of the Holy Spirit, we are guided by the Spirit-inspired Word of God. That's what it means when we read that "All Scripture is breathed out by God and profitable for teaching, for reproof, for correction, and for training in righteousness" (2 Timothy 3:16). When you find yourself cornered by life's challenges, turn to the Bible. Study it deeply, meditate on it, and apply its principles to your life. The Bible offers actionable insights that can help you find God's way out of any difficulty.

Discerning God's Will: The Ongoing Process

Understanding God's will is an ongoing process. It's not a one-time event but a continuous journey. To discern God's will, one must be fully committed to obeying Him and must be keenly aware of the world around them, informed by the Biblical worldview. Often, God's will is reflected in the natural course of events in your life, bounded by the principles and commandments in the Bible. It's like driving on a road with signboards and signals; you need to be aware and attentive to navigate correctly.

The Christian Community: The Importance of Wise Counsel

While God has provided His Word as a guide, He has also placed us in a community of believers for a reason. Seek counsel from spiritually mature Christians who understand the Biblical worldview. There's profound wisdom in the multitude of counselors. As Proverbs 15:22 states, *"Without counsel plans fail, but with many advisers, they succeed."* Wise counsel acts like a second set of eyes that can provide a different perspective grounded in the same Biblical principles.

Application and Action: Walking Through the Open Door

Discerning God's way out isn't merely about intellectual realization; it must be followed by action. You must walk through the door that God has opened. Remember, faith without works is dead (James 2:26). The walk through God's opened door is a walk of faith, but it's also a walk of obedience and action. It's like finding an exit in a maze; once you find it, you must walk through it. You can't just stand there admiring the door.

The Consequence of Choices: There is No Universal Salvation

It's vital to recognize the immense responsibility that comes with free will. God allows us to make choices, but these choices come with consequences. There is no universal salvation. The choices you make today will shape your future and potentially your eternal destiny. There is no 'once saved, always saved' concept. We must endure to the end, continually walking in God's way, to receive the gift of eternal life.

Choosing God's way out is a constant, deliberate act of the will, guided by a love for God and a desire to be obedient to Him.

All Things Work for Good for Those Who Love God

Despite the suffering and trials that we may experience in this world, for those who love God, all things work together for good (Romans 8:28). This doesn't mean that everything that happens to us will be good, but rather that God can use even the bad things for a greater good. By finding and choosing God's way out in our various circumstances, we align ourselves more closely with His sovereign will, ensuring that we are among those who can claim the promise of all things working together for good.

Finding God's way out is a multifaceted endeavor that involves prayer, the study of the Bible, wise counsel from the Christian community, and, most importantly, action. We must be proactive in seeking God's guidance and obeying His commandments to navigate successfully through the maze of life's difficulties, always keeping our eyes on the eternal promise of life in His presence.

CHAPTER 3: The Nature of Doubt and How to Overcome It

The Genesis of Doubt

Doubt is a pervasive experience that permeates the life of almost every believer at some point. Doubt isn't just a fleeting thought; it's more like an invasive weed that, if not addressed, can overrun the garden of your faith. You could liken doubt to a dense fog that obscures the path of truth and leaves you groping for clarity. It's essential to remember that the fog itself isn't the journey; it's a temporary obstruction. Similarly, experiencing doubt doesn't negate your faith; it challenges it.

In the Bible, we find instances where even the most stalwart figures had their moments of doubt. Elijah, who called down fire from heaven, ran away in fear and asked Jehovah to take his life (1 Kings 19). Thomas, one of Jesus' disciples, refused to believe in Christ's resurrection until he saw it for himself (John 20:24-29). These stories show us that doubt is a common human experience, not an unforgivable sin.

Distinguishing Doubt from Unbelief

While doubt and unbelief might seem similar, they are not synonymous. Doubt is a state of uncertainty where belief and disbelief coexist; it's the spiritual equivalent of being at a crossroads. Unbelief, on the other hand, is a definite rejection or neglect of faith. An example can be found in the Israelites' wilderness journey. When they doubted, they asked questions or sought signs. When they disbelieved, they turned to other gods or openly rebelled against Jehovah's commands (Exodus 32; Numbers 14).

Why Doubt Occurs

Several factors contribute to doubt: difficult circumstances, incomplete understanding of God's word, or exposure to differing viewpoints. Picture it like adjusting to a room's lighting after coming in from the glaring sun—you need time to see clearly. Likewise, new or confusing information might require a period of spiritual adjustment.

The Two-Fold Approach to Overcoming Doubt

1. Seek Wisdom through God's Word

The most effective antidote to doubt is the wisdom that comes from God's Word. Scripture itself is replete with verses that speak to our uncertainties. The Apostle Paul says, "So faith comes from hearing, and hearing through the word of Christ" (Romans 10:17). As we dig deep into the Bible, we discover the multi-faceted wisdom of God that can dismantle any root of doubt.

2. Seek Community in the Body of Christ

Being part of a faith community can offer you the emotional and spiritual support you may lack when struggling with doubt. The Bible strongly advocates for communal worship and fellowship (Hebrews 10:25). The shared experiences, testimonies, and teachings within the community help reinforce your faith.

Tackling Specific Doubts

1. Doubt Regarding God's Existence

One of the most basic yet profound doubts is about the existence of God. Yet, the complexity and order of the universe affirm a Creator. The Bible declares, "The heavens declare the glory of God, and the sky above proclaims his handiwork" (Psalms 19:1).

2. Doubt About God's Goodness in Suffering

Another prevalent doubt concerns God's goodness amid suffering. While God didn't design suffering, He allows it to teach humanity an object lesson about the inherent flaws in independence from His sovereignty. In the case of Job, his suffering demonstrated that faith in Jehovah can exist apart from favorable circumstances (Job 1-2).

3. Doubt About Salvation

Many doubt their salvation because they have an erroneous understanding of "once saved, always saved," a concept not supported by Scripture. The Bible makes it clear that one can fall from grace (Hebrews 6:4-6). Our assurance is not in a doctrine but in a person: Jesus Christ, and the relationship we maintain with Him.

Doubt is not a spiritual death sentence; it is a catalyst that can deepen your relationship with God if dealt with properly. Jehovah doesn't despise a questioning heart that genuinely seeks Him. He invites us to reason with Him (Isaiah 1:18). After all, the greatest commandment involves loving God with all our mind (Matthew 22:37). When doubt arises, confront it, don't suppress it. Use doubt as a stepping stone to dive deeper into the endless ocean of God's truth. By doing so, you not only find answers but also develop a resilient faith that stands the test of time.

Identifying Sources of Doubt

Understanding the Phenomenon of Doubt

Doubt is a universal experience, not unique to the Christian walk but magnified within it due to the spiritual stakes involved. It's like a persistent fog that obscures your vision on a journey. Doubt isn't necessarily a sign of weak faith; even the apostle Thomas had his moments of skepticism (John 20:24-29). It's essential to acknowledge that doubt isn't the opposite of faith but rather a hurdle on the pathway of faith.

The Varieties of Doubt: Intellectual and Emotional

Intellectual Doubt stems from questions related to doctrine, Biblical inconsistencies, or the nature of God. Imagine trying to piece together a jigsaw puzzle without having all the pieces; your understanding feels incomplete, leading to skepticism.

Emotional Doubt is often triggered by personal experiences—such as loss or suffering—that make it difficult to reconcile God's goodness. It's like carrying a heavy backpack while trying to climb a steep hill; the extra emotional weight makes the ascent toward faith far more exhausting.

Biblical Perspectives on Doubt

Scripture does not shy away from addressing doubt. In the Old Testament, Job grappled with profound skepticism due to his sufferings. Yet, Jehovah was patient with him, guiding him through his questioning (Job 38-41). In the New Testament, the apostle James encourages believers to ask God for wisdom, assuring that God gives generously to all without finding fault (James 1:5).

Common Sources of Doubt

External Influences

The world is filled with alternative philosophies, worldviews, and even scientific theories that seem to challenge Christian doctrine. It's like standing at a crossroad with numerous signposts pointing in all directions, causing confusion about which way to go.

Internal Struggles

Personal sins or moral failings often lead to doubt. It's a cycle: you sin, you feel unworthy, and then you doubt God's love or your salvation. This vicious circle can be like a merry-go-round that you can't seem to exit.

Theological Misunderstandings

Wrong or incomplete doctrines can also be sources of doubt. For example, misconceptions about the nature of hell can make God seem cruel, thereby fostering doubt about His goodness.

Strategies for Overcoming Doubt

Dive into Scripture

The Bible is our most reliable guide. Like a sturdy ship in stormy seas, it provides the framework for navigating through doubt. Study scripture that speaks directly to your doubts and seek wisdom in its eternal words. Remember 2 Timothy 3:16, which says that all Scripture is God-breathed and useful for teaching and correction.

Engage in Prayer

Prayer is our direct line to God. It's the equivalent of having a heart-to-heart with a trusted friend, laying out all your concerns and questions. Through prayer, we can ask God to strengthen our faith and dispel our doubts.

Seek Wise Counsel

A solo journey through the landscape of doubt can be daunting. Like a traveler consulting a map or asking locals for directions, we can benefit from the wisdom of seasoned believers. Whether it's pastoral guidance or a mature Christian friend, don't underestimate the value of external perspectives.

Evaluate Your Expectations

Sometimes, we doubt because our expectations of God are unrealistic. God allows suffering, but that doesn't make Him uncaring. It's vital to align our expectations with Biblical truth, not human assumptions or desires.

Reaffirming Your Faith Amid Doubt

Doubt does not have to be a dead-end. Think of it as a tunnel that you need to pass through to get to a clearer understanding of your faith. Through conscious efforts like scripture study, prayer, and seeking counsel, you can dispel the fog of doubt and emerge into the light of a stronger belief. While the journey may be challenging, the destination—a deeper, more resilient faith—is undoubtedly worth it.

Scriptures for Combating Doubt

Understanding the Origin of Doubt

When we talk about faith, it is important to remember that it exists on a spectrum. On one end, you have absolute certainty, and on the other, you have crippling doubt. Now, doubt is not inherently evil. In fact, the very nature of faith involves wrestling with doubt. Why? Because faith is the assurance of things we cannot see (Hebrews 11:1). So, when circumstances in life challenge our perception of God's goodness or sovereignty, doubt can creep in. It's like you're sailing on a calm sea and then suddenly, you hit turbulent waters that rock your boat of faith.

What Does the Bible Say About Doubt?

When Thomas, one of the disciples, heard that Jesus had risen, he doubted it until he could touch the wounds of the risen Lord (John 20:24-29). Thomas' doubt was met with a response from Jesus, but not with condemnation. Jehovah God also didn't rebuke Sarah when she laughed in doubt at the idea of having a child in her old age (Genesis 18:12-15). The Bible, therefore, does not shame those who experience doubt but offers pathways for reassurance.

The Role of Satan in Amplifying Doubt

As we live in a world tainted by sin and orchestrated by Satan to some extent, it is no surprise that the "father of lies" would exploit our doubt to pull us away from God. Imagine you're holding a rope, and that rope is your faith. Satan tries to loosen your grip, not usually by a sudden pull, but by slowly and continuously adding weight to the rope. He whispers uncertainties, magnifies your problems, and exploits your fears. He's the noise that drowns out God's whisper, the static in your connection with the divine.

Overcoming Doubt through Scripture

Lean on Jehovah's Everlasting Arms

In moments of doubt, the Old Testament offers solace in the unchanging nature of Jehovah God. Consider the reassurance provided in Isaiah 41:10, "Fear not, for I am with you; be not dismayed, for I am your God; I will strengthen you, I will help you, I will uphold you with my righteous right hand." Jehovah God provides us with his strength, and He doesn't change like shifting shadows.

Let the Life of Jesus Bolster Your Faith

The New Testament provides an abundance of evidence for faith through the life, death, and resurrection of Jesus Christ. As Paul mentioned in Romans 8:32, "He who did not spare his own Son but gave him up for us all, how will he not also with him graciously give us all things?" Jesus' sacrifice is the ultimate testament to God's love for us.

Reflect on God's Past Deliverances

One of the best ways to combat doubt is to remember how God has acted in the past. David often did this by reflecting on God's deliverance from his enemies. It's like looking back at old family photos when you feel lonely or disconnected. They remind you that you're loved, that you belong, and that things can be good again.

Prayer and Honest Conversation with God

It's okay to tell God that you're struggling with doubt. Prayer isn't a one-way street; it's a dialogue. Be like Jacob, who wrestled with God until he received a blessing (Genesis 32:24-30). Your wrestling with doubt isn't a sign of weak faith but an exercise of it.

Stay Connected to the Body of Christ

The church—meaning the people, not the building—is another source of strength in times of doubt. James encourages believers to pray for each other (James 5:16). We need to bear each other's burdens, and sometimes that means helping to carry someone else's doubt while they find their footing in faith again.

Understanding the Nature of Doubt as an Ongoing Struggle

Doubt isn't something that gets "cured." It's an ongoing process. As life changes, new doubts can arise, but the tools for overcoming them remain constant—prayer, scripture, and fellowship. Each time doubt resurfaces, you become better equipped to deal with it. It's like a muscle that gets stronger with exercise.

Doubt is an intricate part of the human experience, even for those with strong faith. Rather than suppressing or ignoring it, the key is to recognize, address, and combat it through the tools God has provided us. Scriptures offer a wealth of guidance and assurance for times of uncertainty, serving as an anchor for our souls when the waves of life try to toss us around. In a world where Satan seeks to exploit our vulnerabilities, leaning on Jehovah's promises and Jesus' sacrifice can fortify our spiritual defenses, helping us to live a life truly "Blessed by God in Satan's World."

The Role of Prayer in Overcoming Doubt

The Weight of Doubt

Doubt is like a stone in your shoe. It's uncomfortable and impedes your walk in faith. If not dealt with, it can cause you to stumble and eventually stop altogether. But we have a loving Father in heaven who wants to help us remove that stone. Before diving into the role of prayer in overcoming doubt, it's crucial to define what doubt is and isn't.

What is Doubt?

In its simplest form, doubt is uncertainty or lack of conviction on issues generally related to faith or trust. However, it's not the same as disbelief or the outright denial of faith. Doubt is more of a questioning, a pause, a desire to understand and be sure. Remember Thomas in the New Testament? He doubted the resurrection of Jesus, saying, "Unless I see in his hands the mark of the nails, and place my finger into the mark of the nails, and place my hand into his side, I will never believe" (John 20:25). Yet when Jesus appeared and dispelled his doubt, Thomas believed.

Unveiling the Sources of Doubt

Think of doubt as the symptom of a deeper issue. Often, doubt arises from intellectual questions, emotional struggles, or spiritual dilemmas. Understanding the source can guide us on how to address it.

Intellectual Doubt

These doubts are more cerebral, often related to logical reasoning or the perceived contradictions in Scripture. For instance, one might doubt the Genesis creation account due to prevailing scientific theories.

Emotional Doubt

These are doubts that stem from emotional states such as grief, loneliness, or fear. If God is good, why did He allow this suffering? Emotional doubt is usually temporary but can be spiritually paralyzing if not addressed.

Spiritual Doubt

Spiritual doubt pertains to one's relationship with God. Can God forgive me? Does He still love me despite my sins? These doubts often involve personal feelings of unworthiness.

The Role of Prayer in Overcoming Doubt

Prayer is our direct line to God, a way to bring our questions and concerns to Him who knows all things. But prayer isn't just about talking; it's also about listening and being still in the presence of God. Here's how prayer can help us tackle the different types of doubts:

For Intellectual Doubt

By engaging God in prayer, we ask for wisdom and understanding. James 1:5 says, "If any of you lacks wisdom, let him ask God, who gives generously to all without reproach, and it will be given him." Through prayer, we can be led to resources, teachings, and Scriptural passages that help reconcile our intellectual conflicts.

For Emotional Doubt

In times of emotional turmoil, prayer provides a therapeutic channel to pour out our hearts to God. The psalmist did this frequently, especially in times of desperation. "I pour out my complaint before him; I tell my trouble before him" (Psalm 142:2).

For Spiritual Doubt

When we doubt our standing with God, prayer becomes an avenue for realignment and reassurance. Through prayer, we can confess, and God, who is faithful, will forgive us (1 John 1:9). It's like a spiritual reset button, a fresh start in our relationship with Him.

Practices for Effective Prayer

Consistency and Patience

Treat prayer as a daily conversation with God. Keep the lines open and be patient for His answers.

Prayerful Study of the Word

The Bible is often described as God's love letter to us. Prayerful study of His Word provides divine insights and addresses doubts grounded in ignorance or misunderstanding of Scripture.

Communal Prayer

There's added strength in communal prayers. When two or more are gathered in His name, God promises to be in their midst (Matthew 18:20).

Doubt is not an unpardonable sin nor a permanent state. It is a challenge to our faith, one that we can overcome through the divine tool of prayer. As we lay our doubts before God, let's remember that faith is not the absence of doubt but the choice to trust God despite it. *Therefore let us draw near with confidence to the throne of grace, so that we may receive mercy and find grace to help in time of need* (Hebrews 4:16).

Edward D. Andrews

CHAPTER 4: What Is Faith and How to Examine Yours

The Essence of Faith

Faith is more than mere belief. It's a complex structure, combining trust, confidence, and action. Hebrews 11:1 explains, "Now faith is the assurance of things hoped for, the conviction of things not seen." Faith doesn't rely on physical proof but is confident in the unseen realities because of trust in Jehovah and His Word. Think of it like investing in a startup. You can't see immediate profits, but you invest based on trust in the vision and team. So, too, faith is our investment in God's promises, a trust we enact through living in line with His guidance.

Understanding Genuine Faith

James 2:17 drives home the point, stating, "So also faith by itself, if it does not have works, is dead." It's not enough to simply say we believe in Jesus Christ; our actions must demonstrate our faith. Just as a car needs fuel to move, our faith needs works to be alive. Otherwise, it's as if we're driving a car that's stuck in neutral.

Test Your Faith: Self-Examination

Paul tells us in 2 Corinthians 13:5, "Examine yourselves, to see whether you are in the faith. Test yourselves." Self-examination isn't a one-time event but a continuous process. Think of it as a spiritual health check-up. Here's how you can do it:

Biblical Understanding

First, check whether your beliefs align with the Bible's teachings. Many stray because they lean on human philosophies rather than Biblical truth.

Conduct and Lifestyle

Next, examine your conduct. Your actions should be a reflection of Christ's teachings. Are you emulating the fruits of the spirit mentioned in Galatians 5:22-23?

Relationship with God

Your personal relationship with God is also a crucial aspect. Like any relationship, it requires communication—prayer and Bible study are key components. You wouldn't expect a friendship to thrive without conversation, and the same goes for your relationship with God.

Love for Others

Jesus states in John 13:35, "By this all people will know that you are my disciples, if you have love for one another." If you don't have love for others, that's a sign to re-examine your faith.

The Dangers of Shallow Faith

Shallow faith is like a plant in poor soil; it may sprout but will eventually wither. Matthew 13:20-21 warns against this: "As for what was sown on rocky ground, this is the one who hears the word and immediately receives it with joy, yet he has no root in himself, but endures for a while, and when tribulation or persecution arises on account of the word, immediately he falls away." Beware of letting emotions alone drive your faith. Emotions can be as shifting as sand and cannot sustain you in trials or tribulations.

Robust Faith in a World of Skepticism

We live in a world increasingly skeptical of religious convictions. First Peter 3:15 urges us to "always be prepared to make a defense to anyone who asks you for a reason for the hope that is in you; yet do it with gentleness and respect." If someone were to ask you why you believe what you do, could you give a Biblically sound answer? Strong faith can stand up to scrutiny and provide light in a world of skepticism.

Counterfeit Faith: Be Alert

Just as there are counterfeit currencies, there are counterfeit forms of faith. Many claim to be followers of Christ, yet their lives reflect something different. First John 2:4 warns, "Whoever says 'I know him' but does not keep his commandments is a liar, and the truth is not in him." False faith is deceptive because it has the appearance of authenticity without the substance.

Strengthening Your Faith

Strengthening your faith is an ongoing process and involves continuous study of God's Word, prayer, and living a life in alignment with Biblical principles. Romans 10:17 states, "So faith comes from hearing, and hearing through the word of Christ." It's like exercise for your soul—consistent spiritual exercise makes your faith stronger.

The Imperative of Faith for Salvation

Faith is not an optional extra in the Christian life; it's essential for salvation. Ephesians 2:8-9 affirms this, "For by grace you have been saved through faith. And this is not your own doing; it is the gift of God, not a result of works, so that no one may boast." There's no other route to salvation. However, remember that faith without works is dead. In this context, works are not to earn salvation but to demonstrate authentic faith.

Faith is not just an abstract concept but a vital part of our Christian walk. A genuine faith stands as a living, active force in our lives. It is nurtured by a deep understanding of the Bible, evidenced by a Christ-like lifestyle, and fortified against the dangers of false or shallow faith. Being proactive in examining and nurturing your faith ensures that you remain rooted in Christ, ready to thrive even in a world that might be hostile to your beliefs.

The Biblical Definition of Faith

Setting the Stage for Understanding Faith

Faith is a term that appears quite frequently in religious and secular conversations alike. Yet its definition, especially its biblical definition, is often misunderstood or inadequately explained. In the context of the Bible, faith is not a mere emotional sentiment or a blind leap into the unknown. Instead, it is a robust principle that touches every aspect of Christian life. Understanding what the Bible really says about faith can provide clarity and depth to our relationship with God.

Faith as Trust

The most straightforward definition of biblical faith can be found in Hebrews 11:1: "Now faith is the assurance of things hoped for, the conviction of things not seen." In simple terms, faith is a trust in what you cannot physically verify. Just as you might trust that a chair will hold you up even before you sit on it, faith involves trust in God's promises even if you can't see the outcome right away. However, this trust is not a passive expectation; it is an active reliance on God. Trusting God means entrusting our lives, hopes, and future into His hands.

Faith as Knowledge-based

The Bible's presentation of faith is never that of blind trust. The faith described in Scriptures is rooted in knowledge and understanding of God's character and His promises. Romans 10:17 declares, "So faith comes from hearing, and hearing through the word of Christ." Here, we see that faith is not separate from reason or knowledge but is actually built upon it. The more you know about God, the more substantial your faith becomes. It's like a relationship; the more you know about a person, the more you can trust them. In God's case, we come to know Him through His revealed Word, and our trust deepens as our knowledge increases.

Faith as Commitment

Faith in the biblical sense goes beyond merely believing in God's existence. It includes a commitment to follow Him. James 2:19 warns, "You believe that God is one; you do well. Even the demons believe—and shudder!" Merely acknowledging God's existence is not enough; even the demons do that. Biblical faith involves making a commitment to trust and follow God. It's like deciding to get married; the commitment doesn't stop at the wedding ceremony. It's a lifelong promise of trust, loyalty, and fidelity.

Faith as Relational

In essence, faith is relational. It is not merely an intellectual acknowledgment or a blind trust but a relational trust and commitment to God. Think of it like a friendship. In a genuine friendship, you have knowledge of who your friend is, trust based on your experiences together, and a commitment to maintaining the relationship. Similarly, faith involves knowing God (intellectual aspect), trusting God (emotional aspect), and committing to God (volitional aspect).

Faith in Practice: Living Out Faith

Living out faith means acting according to God's will, even when it's challenging. Abraham, often considered the father of faith, provides an excellent example. He left his home, not knowing where he was going, simply because God told him to. Even when God asked him to sacrifice his son Isaac, Abraham's faith did not waver. He trusted that God had a plan and was committed to following it, no matter the cost. His faith was not just a mental acceptance of facts but an active, lived-out trust.

Faith as Ongoing

Faith is not a one-time event; it is ongoing and grows over time. The apostle Paul mentioned "fighting the good fight of faith" in 1 Timothy 6:12. This implies that faith involves struggle, challenge, and continual growth. Like a muscle that strengthens with use, faith grows through testing, trials, and the daily decision to trust God. Even when we stumble, our ongoing faith means that we turn back to God, asking for forgiveness and resolving to trust Him more fully.

Faith and Salvation: An Inseparable Pair

One of the most pivotal roles of faith is in the matter of salvation. Ephesians 2:8-9 tells us, "For by grace you have been saved through faith. And this is not your own doing; it is the gift of God, not a result of works, so that no one may boast." Faith is the means by which we accept the grace of God in salvation. It is not mere belief but an active, ongoing, relational trust and commitment to God. And while salvation is a gift from God, our faith allows us to accept and live out that gift daily.

The Comprehensive Nature of Biblical Faith

Biblical faith is a multi-faceted concept that cannot be easily reduced to a single definition. It involves trust, knowledge, commitment, a relational dimension, practical application, and ongoing growth. It is the backbone of the Christian life and the means by which we enter into and maintain a relationship with God. As we deepen our understanding of what biblical faith truly is, we are better equipped to live out a meaningful and committed Christian life.

Self-examination: Are You in the Faith?

The Urgency of Self-Examination

Paul, the Apostle to the Gentiles, urges Christians to "Examine yourselves, to see whether you are in the faith. Test yourselves" (2 Corinthians 13:5. Self-examination is not a mere recommendation; it is an essential exercise for spiritual health. Imagine you're driving a car. You wouldn't ignore the dashboard lights indicating low fuel or an engine issue. Your spiritual life has its indicators that require your attention.

Understanding What "In the Faith" Means

Being "in the faith" isn't just about identifying as a Christian or going to church. It's like having a valid ticket for a long journey. The ticket is your faith, based on accurate knowledge and genuine relationship with God through Christ. It is the quality of this ticket—your faith—that needs regular examination.

The Role of Works and Faith

James pointedly says, "faith by itself, if it is not accompanied by action, is dead" (James 2:17). This doesn't mean that we earn salvation through works. Instead, think of works as the fruit that naturally grows from the tree of faith. If the tree is healthy, good fruit will come naturally. The absence of fruit signals a problem with the tree.

Regular Introspection and Repentance

David prayed, "Search me, O God, and know my heart!" (Psalm 139:23). If King David, described as "a man after God's own heart," felt the need for divine scrutiny, how much more do we? A vital part of this self-examination is repentance. Unlike general regret, repentance is a change of direction, a turn toward God. It's like making a U-turn when you realize you're going the wrong way.

The Perils of Self-Deception

It's shockingly easy to deceive ourselves, thinking we're in the faith when we're not. Jesus warns about those who will claim to have done miracles in His name but to whom He will declare, "I never knew you; depart from me, you workers of lawlessness" (Matthew 7:23). To avoid this terrifying scenario, one needs to engage in honest self-assessment regularly. Picture this as a mirror that shows not your physical appearance but your spiritual state. A mirror doesn't lie; it shows things as they are. Likewise, honest self-examination brings clarity.

The Litmus Test of Love

Jesus gave a new commandment: "love one another: just as I have loved you" (John 13:34). This is not merely a sentimental love but involves practical sacrifices and care for others. A critical indicator of being in the faith is our love for fellow believers and even our enemies. If you find this challenging, imagine your heart as a garden. Love is a plant that should naturally grow there. If it doesn't, you need to investigate the soil's condition—your heart.

The Word as a Guide, Not Emotions

Our feelings are like weather—constantly changing. Hence, the objective Word of God must be our guide. When the Bible says, "Your word is a lamp to my feet and a light to my path" (Psalm 119:105), it implies that we navigate our spiritual life through the objective Word, not subjective emotions. Think of the Bible as your spiritual GPS. If it signals that you're going off course, take corrective action immediately.

The Community of Believers

Being in the faith is not a solo endeavor. We are part of a body, the church, and we must function as such. If you're in a genuine relationship with God, you'll naturally desire fellowship with His people. Imagine a coal separated from the burning embers; it quickly loses its heat. Likewise, the isolated Christian becomes spiritually cold.

The Dangers of Spiritual Complacency

One of the dangers that even long-time Christians face is spiritual complacency. In the book of Revelation, the church in Laodicea is criticized for being "neither cold nor hot" (Revelation 3:15). Complacency is a sign that one may not be in the faith as strongly as assumed. It's like becoming careless in driving just because you've been doing it for years. The stakes are too high to allow such negligence.

The Assurance of Self-Examination

The good news is that regular, honest self-examination can give you a reliable assurance of your standing before God. Paul, after exhorting the Corinthians to examine themselves, expresses his confidence that they will do nothing wrong (2 Corinthians 13:7). Similarly, this self-examination will lead to necessary adjustments and a strengthened relationship with God.

The Continuous Journey of Self-Examination

Being in the faith is a dynamic relationship, not a static condition. Like any meaningful relationship, it requires constant attention and regular check-ups. The rewards for taking self-examination seriously are immense, ensuring that we stay on the narrow path that leads to eternal life. It allows us to be not merely hearers of the Word but doers, actively participating in God's plans and enjoying His blessings.

This is not a one-time event but a lifelong process, ensuring that your faith is not just an inherited tradition or a cultural identity but a vibrant, growing relationship with the living God. Let us heed Paul's advice earnestly. Let us examine ourselves, test ourselves, and thereby solidify our place in the faith.

Growing in Faith Through Difficult Times

Life is filled with peaks and valleys, and for the Christian, these challenging seasons serve not as a sign of God's absence, but as an arena for faith to be stretched, tested, and ultimately strengthened. Understanding how to grow in faith through difficult times requires diving into the Holy Scriptures for wisdom, resilience, and hope.

The Nature of Difficult Times

First, we need to acknowledge that living in a fallen world means we will encounter hardships. While God didn't design suffering to foster growth, He allows it. As Christians, we understand that this is a result of human independence from God's sovereignty (Note 14). The Bible is clear that "we must through much tribulation enter into the kingdom of God" (Acts 14:22). The Apostle Paul himself faced numerous trials but used them as a way to demonstrate the sufficiency of God's grace (2 Cor. 12:9).

Faith as Trust in God's Sovereignty

At its core, faith is trust. In the midst of adversity, do you trust God? Trusting in God's sovereignty means recognizing that God has allowed difficulties for a purpose. Though we may not fully understand why suffering exists, we believe that God's plans are to prosper us and not to harm us (Jer. 29:11). Think of it like navigation: you may not see the entire path from your starting point, but you trust that following the GPS will get you to your destination. Similarly, God's Word serves as our spiritual GPS.

God's Word as the Cornerstone of Faith

To navigate through the hardships of life, you'll need a solid foundation. Your faith should be rooted in the Word of God, the Bible. The apostle Paul said, "So faith comes from hearing, and hearing through the word of Christ" (Rom. 10:17). God's Word equips you with the spiritual tools needed to confront any obstacles you face.

Overcoming the Temptation to Doubt

In the face of adversity, doubt can easily creep in. However, doubt is not the absence of faith but a hurdle in its path. Remember the father who asked Jesus to heal his son in Mark 9:24, "I believe; help my unbelief!" This captures the complex relationship between faith and doubt. Pray for God to help you overcome your unbelief, just as this father did.

Praying for Strength and Wisdom

The power of prayer should not be underestimated during tough times. James encourages us, "If any of you lacks wisdom, let him ask

God, who gives generously to all without reproach, and it will be given him" (James 1:5). Prayer is not just a spiritual exercise; it's a lifeline to the Almighty Jehovah. Consider it your direct line of communication with the control tower while navigating through a storm.

Emotional Honesty and Vulnerability with God

David, the man after God's own heart, was no stranger to despair. Yet, he was also emotionally honest before Jehovah. We too can approach God with our raw feelings, doubts, and questions. The Psalms are filled with anguished cries, desperate pleas, and yet, expressions of unwavering hope in God. Your relationship with God can withstand your tough questions and emotional pain.

The Role of Christian Community

Though faith is personal, it's not meant to be private. The New Testament often talks about the importance of the Christian community. Fellow believers are there to encourage you, share burdens, and offer wisdom (Gal. 6:2; Heb. 10:24-25). If you're struggling in your faith, don't isolate yourself. Reach out to trusted believers who can provide biblical counsel and prayerful support.

Future Hope: A Motivating Factor

Finally, the anticipation of eternal life gives us the strength to endure current suffering. As Paul says, "For this light momentary affliction is preparing for us an eternal weight of glory beyond all comparison" (2 Cor. 4:17). The trials of today are shaping us for a glorious future that far outweighs them.

In conclusion, difficult times are a part of life, yet they offer fertile ground for faith to grow. By leaning into God's sovereignty, immersing ourselves in His Word, confronting our doubts, and availing ourselves of prayer and community, we can navigate these challenging seasons with a steadfast faith. And in doing so, we honor God and prepare ourselves for the eternal glory that awaits us.

CHAPTER 5: How All Things Work Together for Your Good

The Sovereign Hand in a Chaotic World

In a world filled with hardship, injustice, and evil, it's a stretch for some to believe that "all things work together for good." However, it is crucial to understand this not as a cliché but as a divinely-ordained truth rooted in Scripture. "And we know that for those who love God all things work together for good, for those who are called according to his purpose" (Romans 8:28). This verse encapsulates the idea but needs unpacking.

God's Sovereignty

In the Bible, Jehovah is described as the Sovereign Ruler of the universe. His sovereignty is not random or capricious, but purposeful. He allows events to unfold and even permits suffering, not because He delights in our pain, but because He aims for a greater good. Think of it like a master artist, crafting a mosaic where every tiny, broken shard eventually forms a masterpiece. Each event in your life—good or bad—is a single piece of a far larger picture.

Working Together: The Divine Orchestration

Interconnected Events

Life often appears to be a series of unconnected events, like dots on a paper. However, God, being outside of time and possessing foreknowledge of all things, can connect these dots in a way that produces an outcome for our good. It's like a filmmaker expertly editing scenes so that the final movie is a masterpiece.

Embracing the Inexplicable

Sometimes things happen that we simply can't explain. Job, a man described as "blameless" and "upright," suffered tremendously. Yet, through that suffering, he drew closer to God, developed perseverance, and his faith was refined. Even in inexplicable circumstances, God's design is at work.

The Necessity of Free Will

Our Choices Matter

Free will is not an illusion but a reality that has both blessings and consequences. Yet, God's foreknowledge enables Him to factor in our decisions to bring about His purposes. It's not that He controls our decisions, but that He integrates them into His divine plan. Imagine a chess grandmaster playing against a novice; the grandmaster doesn't control the novice's moves but can still predict them and plan many moves ahead.

The Realities of Suffering

Suffering Is Not a Divine Plan but a Divine Allowance

It's a common misunderstanding to think that God creates suffering to teach us lessons. Instead, God allows suffering as part of the human experience and the consequence of living in a fallen world. It is an object lesson that teaches us the dangers of independence from God's sovereignty. Though He doesn't design suffering, He uses it for our good.

The Greater Good in Suffering

Joseph's life serves as a vivid example. Sold into slavery by his brothers, wrongly accused, and imprisoned—his life was a series of unfortunate events. Yet at the end of it all, he could say to his brothers, "You meant evil against me, but God meant it for good" (Genesis 50:20). Through his suffering, not only was Joseph personally refined, but he also ended up saving many lives.

The Eternal Perspective

The Weight of Glory

The apostle Paul writes that "this light momentary affliction is preparing for us an eternal weight of glory beyond all comparison" (2 Corinthians 4:17). Our lives on Earth are like a drop in the ocean compared to eternity. Sometimes it takes an eternal perspective to see how our temporary struggles contribute to our everlasting good.

Salvation: The Ultimate Good

The ultimate manifestation of all things working together for good is the redemptive work of Jesus Christ. His life, death, and resurrection were not isolated events but a series of divinely-orchestrated moments that culminated in the offer of salvation for humanity. Without the Fall, there would be no need for Redemption. Without death, there would be no resurrection. Without sin, there would be no Savior.

The Boundaries: Who Does It Apply To?

Specific to Those Who Love God

It's important to clarify that the promise of all things working together for good is specific to those "who love God, to those who are called according to His purpose" (Romans 8:28). It is not a universal promise but applies only to those in a right relationship with God through Christ.

In a world that often feels like it's under the sway of chaos and darkness, the divine promise stands unshakable. Jehovah, the Sovereign Ruler, meticulously works all things together for the good of those who love Him. This isn't a cosmic accident but a divinely orchestrated plan. While we may not always see or understand how every piece fits, we can trust that the Master Artist is creating a masterpiece with our lives.

So, in a world where Satan seems to be in control, remember that he's merely a usurper. Jehovah God remains the ultimate Sovereign, and in His wisdom and love, He ensures that all things—even the painful and perplexing—work together for our good.

The Truth in Romans 8:28

Romans 8:28 is often cited as a comforting verse, especially in times of distress. It states, "And we know that for those who love God all things work together for good, for those who are called according to his purpose." This verse seems to offer assurance that even in dire circumstances, God is working things out for our benefit. But what does this promise truly mean? Let's dive deep into the text to uncover the profound truths hidden in this oft-quoted verse.

Context Matters: Setting the Stage

Understanding the broader context in which Romans 8:28 is found is crucial. The apostle Paul, the author of Romans, was addressing the early Christians in Rome. These Christians were not strangers to suffering. They lived in an environment hostile to their faith, and yet Paul encouraged them with the assurance that their present trials were not in vain. By stating that "all things work together for good," Paul was not presenting a superficial view of life's challenges but offering a deep, spiritually enriched perspective grounded in the reality of God's sovereign plan.

The Components of the Promise

"All Things"

When Paul says "all things," he means precisely that. Whether it is suffering, persecution, or even the mundane aspects of life, God is working through all circumstances. Unlike a potter limited by the quality of clay, God is so sovereign and powerful that He uses even the "bad clay" to make something beautiful.

"Work Together"

The phrase "work together" signifies a synergistic operation. It is not that each event in your life independently contributes to your good. Rather, God orchestrates a plethora of experiences, decisions, and events to collectively serve a divine purpose. Like a master conductor leading a symphony, every instrument—though different—plays a part in creating a harmonious sound.

"For Good"

The term "for good" does not necessarily mean immediate happiness or relief from suffering. The "good" in view here is likely much more profound. It is good defined on God's terms, which often focuses on our spiritual maturity, character development, and ultimately, our eternal joy.

"For Those Who Love God" and "Are Called According to His Purpose"

This promise is not a universal guarantee. It is specifically aimed at "those who love God" and are "called according to his purpose." In other words, this is a promise for the believers, those who have entered into a saving relationship with Jesus Christ and are walking in line with God's will.

Free Will and God's Sovereignty

The question often arises: if God is sovereign, what about our free will? The concept of God orchestrating "all things for good" in no way negates human freedom or accountability. In His foreknowledge, God knows all the potentialities of free will decisions. This foreknowledge is not restrictive but all-encompassing, allowing God to achieve His purposes without violating human freedom.

The Grand Tapestry of God's Plan

Consider your life as a tapestry. Each thread represents an event, decision, or circumstance. When you look at a single thread in isolation, it might appear insignificant or even ugly. However, when you step back and see the tapestry as a whole, orchestrated by the master weaver, you begin to appreciate how every thread has contributed to a beautiful design. This is what Romans 8:28 promises—a grand tapestry where everything has its place and purpose.

Eternal Perspective

When Paul penned Romans 8:28, he was not offering a quick-fix solution to life's problems. The promise that "all things work together for good" can only be fully understood through an eternal lens. The "good" might not manifest immediately; it might only make sense in the light of eternity. It is the assurance of this final and ultimate good that gives us the courage to persevere through the trials of today.

Romans 8:28 is not a magic formula that makes all problems disappear. Rather, it is a profound theological statement that should anchor us in times of storm. It assures us that no matter what we face, we are under the watchful, sovereign care of a God who loves us and is powerful enough to turn all things for our ultimate good. This verse encourages us to lean into our faith, even more, when the winds of life are blowing hardest against us. It teaches us to see our life's events, no matter how difficult or mundane, as threads in a grand, divine tapestry that God is weaving for our good and His glory.

Real-life Examples of Trials Turning to Triumphs

The Purpose Behind the Struggle

Life in our broken world inevitably comes with its share of trials and tribulations. Yet, as the Apostle Paul wisely counseled, "we know that for those who love God all things work together for good" (Romans 8:28). Indeed, even though God didn't design suffering, He allows it as an object lesson, demonstrating the folly of human independence from His sovereignty. With that in mind, let's consider historical figures in the Christian faith who faced great adversity, yet their trials led to remarkable triumphs that significantly impacted Christianity.

William Tyndale: The Cost of Making the Bible Accessible

William Tyndale, a name synonymous with the English Bible, was a man who faced incredible opposition for the sake of making the Scriptures accessible. Born around 1494 C.E., Tyndale was well-educated and had a fervor for biblical truth. This enthusiasm led him to an audacious task: translating the Bible into English, an act considered heretical at the time.

Persecution soon followed Tyndale like a shadow. The church authorities vehemently opposed his work, forcing him to flee England and live most of his life as a fugitive. However, his adversity proved to be the soil from which sprouted the seeds of a biblical reformation. Tyndale's English translation laid the foundation for the various versions of the Bible we have today. His pioneering work has made it possible for millions to read the Scriptures in a language they can understand. He was executed for heresy in 1536 C.E., but his impact on Christianity was, and still is, monumental. Tyndale's life teaches us that sometimes the path to spiritual triumph involves earthly trials, and even earthly defeat.

Martin Luther: Wrestling with Faith and Starting a Reformation

Another transformative figure in Christian history is Martin Luther. A monk troubled by the church's unbiblical practices, Luther sought righteousness through works but found no peace in his efforts. His trial was internal, a struggle with doubt, guilt, and fear. Yet, this emotional and spiritual struggle led him to a deep study of the Scriptures.

His turning point came upon studying Romans 1:17, "For in it the righteousness of God is revealed from faith for faith, as it is written, 'The righteous shall live by faith.'" This realization changed Luther's perspective completely and led to the 95 Theses, which sparked the Protestant Reformation. Luther faced excommunication, lived under the ban of the Emperor, and was often in physical danger. However, his trials led to a triumph that reshaped the Christian landscape by aligning church doctrine more closely with the Scriptures.

Harriet Tubman: Faith in the Face of Slavery

Moving ahead a few centuries, we encounter Harriet Tubman, born into slavery in the early 1800s C.E. While not a religious leader, her Christian faith was the driving force behind her extraordinary efforts to free slaves through the Underground Railroad. Facing unimaginable hardship and danger, she leaned on her faith in God, whom she often credited for her successful missions. Her life stands as a testament to how faith can lead to triumph in the most dire of circumstances. Her struggle against slavery was a perilous endeavor, yet her trust in God made her an instrument for the liberation of hundreds.

Dietrich Bonhoeffer: Resistance Through Faith

Dietrich Bonhoeffer, a German pastor and theologian, presents another poignant example of trials turning to triumphs. Born in 1906 C.E., Bonhoeffer opposed the corrupting influence of Nazism on the German Church and was involved in efforts to resist Hitler. His involvement in a plot to assassinate Hitler led to his arrest and eventual execution in 1945 C.E.

Though he died at a young age, his writings, especially works like "The Cost of Discipleship," have had a lasting impact on Christian theology and the notion of costly grace. Bonhoeffer's life serves as a lesson that sometimes the ultimate triumph is standing firm in faith, even when facing death.

The Tapestry of Trials and Triumphs

It's not a coincidence that many heroes of the faith endured trials that most would consider insurmountable. While God allows suffering, He also uses the struggles to achieve divine purposes, even if we don't see it immediately. The lives of William Tyndale, Martin Luther, Harriet Tubman, and Dietrich Bonhoeffer demonstrate that trials are often the precursor to triumphs that have far-reaching effects for the kingdom of God.

As we navigate our journey through a world steeped in adversity, let us draw inspiration from these luminaries. Though their trials were immense, the resulting triumphs were monumental. Let us remain steadfast, knowing that if we love God and are called according to His purpose, all things will indeed work for our good.

Trusting God's Sovereignty

The Definition of Sovereignty

Let's start by clarifying what sovereignty means in a theological context. **God's sovereignty refers to His ultimate, supreme authority over the universe.** It means He has the power to accomplish His will and purpose, even though we have the free will to make choices. God's sovereignty is not a matter of forcing or compelling, but rather orchestrating and permitting.

Imagine a skilled conductor leading an orchestra. He doesn't play each instrument himself; he directs the musicians, who have free will and the choice to follow his guidance or not. Similarly, God allows us to make choices, but He's the ultimate conductor, ensuring the outcome aligns with His grand design.

The Balance Between God's Sovereignty and Human Free Will

One common struggle is reconciling God's sovereignty with human free will. **We have the freedom to make choices, but these choices operate within the framework of God's divine plan.** It's not a cosmic puppet show where God pulls all the strings, nor is it a free-for-all where God has abdicated His throne. It's a nuanced relationship that respects both God's sovereignty and our free agency.

Imagine a river that flows toward a destination (God's sovereign will). You're in a canoe (your life), and you have a paddle (your free will). You can paddle left or right, fast or slow, but the river's current

(God's sovereignty) is always influencing your direction. You can make choices, but you can't change the river's ultimate destination.

Why Trusting in God's Sovereignty Matters

Trusting in God's sovereignty is essential because it affects how we respond to life's challenges and opportunities. Whether you are facing health issues, financial crises, or relational difficulties, understanding that God is in control helps you navigate through the ups and downs. Remember Job? He went through unimaginable suffering, yet he stated, "Though he slay me, I will hope in him" (Job 13:15). Job had a deep-rooted belief in the sovereignty of God, even in the darkest of circumstances.

Suffering and God's Sovereignty

It's a challenging subject but crucial to address. The issue isn't that God *designed* suffering, as some might argue. Rather, He *permits* suffering as a part of the larger framework of our fallen world. Think of a parent who permits a child to touch a hot stove after repeated warnings. The child learns a painful but valuable lesson. In a similar fashion, suffering serves as an object lesson to humanity. It may not be a direct cause-and-effect relationship, but it aligns within the framework of God's sovereignty.

The Role of Faith in Understanding Sovereignty

Believing in God's sovereignty requires an element of faith. We cannot see the full picture, but we have faith that God does. Just as a single brushstroke is part of a grand masterpiece, our lives—complete with joys and hardships—are a part of God's ultimate plan.

"Trust in the Lord with all your heart, and do not lean on your own understanding. In all your ways acknowledge him, and he will make straight your paths" (Proverbs 3:5-6). These verses encapsulate the essence of trusting in God's sovereignty. Our limited understanding may raise questions or doubts, but acknowledging

God's supreme authority reassures us that we are part of something far greater than ourselves.

Practical Steps in Trusting God's Sovereignty

So, how do you practically trust God's sovereignty on a daily basis? First, **start your day by surrendering your will to God.** This sets the tone for the day and aligns your perspective with His. Second, **turn your worries into prayers.** Instead of agonizing over your circumstances, elevate them to God, who's in control. Third, **dive into the Scriptures.** Passages that emphasize God's sovereignty serve as a daily reminder of His control over our lives.

CHAPTER 6: Drawing Closer to God Amidst Difficulties

The Crucible of Suffering

Suffering is a ubiquitous aspect of human existence. None escape its grip, and for many, the question isn't whether they will suffer but when and how. The Scriptures affirm that suffering is a reality of life. As Job, a man who endured enormous hardship, put it, "Man who is born of a woman is few of days and full of trouble" (Job 14:1). Despite the pain and emotional turmoil suffering often brings, it can serve as an opportunity to draw closer to God. Why would a loving God permit suffering? Far from a sign of God's indifference or inability, suffering is allowed by Him as an object lesson—teaching humanity about the importance of His sovereignty and the consequences of human rebellion.

Understanding God's Permissiveness Toward Suffering

Some wonder why a loving God would allow suffering in the first place. It's essential to note that God didn't design suffering for growth or endurance; rather, He permits it to manifest the inherent flaws in human independence from His rule. It's as if He is saying, "You want to know what life looks like without my governance? Here it is." Thus, life becomes a classroom where the bitter consequences of sin serve as poignant lessons about our need for divine guidance and our incapability to govern ourselves.

Strengthening Faith During Hard Times

Faith is like a muscle. For it to grow, it needs to be exercised. Hard times can act like a gym for your faith, providing you with the resistance needed to strengthen your trust in God. While suffering, many find solace in God's Word. Scriptures such as Romans 5:3-4, which states, "we rejoice in our sufferings, knowing that suffering produces endurance, and endurance produces character, and character produces hope," can offer profound encouragement. In this analogy, enduring through hardships equates to completing a set of challenging exercises. The result is spiritual stamina that enables us to endure future hardships while holding steadfast in our faith.

Prayer as the Linchpin

Prayer is often described as the lifeblood of a Christian's relationship with God. Think of prayer as a direct line to the Almighty. When you're going through difficulties, instead of allowing despair to sever that line, use it to draw closer to Him. In Philippians 4:6-7, Paul instructs, "do not be anxious about anything, but in everything by prayer and supplication with thanksgiving let your requests be made known to God." With this heavenly communication channel open, we not only express our anxieties and fears but also position ourselves to listen to God's counsel through His Word and conscience-formed wisdom.

Realizing God's Unchanging Nature

One crucial aspect of drawing close to God during trials is recognizing His unchanging nature. Despite our changing circumstances, God remains the same—forever faithful and loving. Like a mountain that stands tall irrespective of the weather conditions around it, God's character is stable. This realization can be a source of immense comfort, as Malachi 3:6 affirms, "For I, Jehovah, do not change."

God's Word as Your Compass

The Bible is more than a collection of ancient manuscripts; it's the inspired guidebook for life, provided by God Himself. In times of suffering, it can offer a roadmap out of despair. The Psalms are often a refuge for the afflicted soul, providing both an expression of sorrow and a reminder of God's goodness. For example, Psalm 34:18 declares, "Jehovah is nigh unto them that are of a broken heart, And saveth such as are of a contrite spirit." These aren't just nice words; they are spiritual landmarks pointing the way through the rocky terrains of life.

Understanding the Role of Community

As humans, we are not solitary beings. Our emotional and spiritual health is often tied to the community we belong to. The New Testament frequently uses the metaphor of a body to describe the church. Just as a human body relies on different parts to function correctly, so the body of Christ operates most effectively when each member plays their role. Therefore, in times of suffering, the community of believers can be a crucial support system. The Apostle Paul counsels us to "bear one another's burdens, and so fulfill the law of Christ" (Galatians 6:2).

Reorienting Our Perspective

Drawing close to God during difficulties may require a shift in perspective. Instead of asking "why me?" one might start asking "what can I learn?" Such a perspective is rooted in the sovereignty of God, acknowledging that our earthly troubles are temporary but have the potential to produce enduring spiritual fruit.

Conclusion: Navigating Through the Storm

Suffering is a complex and multifaceted issue that provokes questions, doubts, and fears. Nevertheless, it also serves as an avenue to deepen our relationship with God. Through prayer, reliance on God's Word, community, and a reorientation of our perspective, we can navigate the turbulent waters of adversity. With God as the Captain of our ship, we can find solace in the midst of suffering and emerge from it with a strengthened faith and a deeper intimacy with our Creator.

The Principle of James 4:8

James 4:8 is a call to action, urging believers to draw near to God, with the assurance that God will, in turn, draw near to them. This powerful principle encapsulates the essence of what a relationship with God is about—closeness, intimacy, and mutual engagement. To help us understand the profound richness and applicability of James 4:8, let's examine it through the following facets:

The Contextual Landscape

Understanding the context in which James wrote this message enhances its value. James addresses a Christian audience facing various trials and temptations, including disputes and disunity. In a sense, they were far from God in their behaviors and attitudes, consumed by worldly desires. James 4:8 serves as a spiritual compass, guiding the believers back to the right path.

What It Means to "Draw Near"

To "draw near" is not a mere physical relocation but a heartfelt, spiritual approach towards God. It's akin to a child reaching out to their parent, seeking comfort, guidance, and love. Here, the term 'draw near' encapsulates the whole being—mind, heart, and soul.

For Example: It's like a close friendship. In a real friendship, both parties make an effort to get to know each other better, to spend time together, and to support each other in times of need. If you don't make the effort, the relationship stagnates.

The Call to Purity

James not only calls his audience to draw near to God but also sets prerequisites: "Cleanse your hands, you sinners, and purify your hearts, you double-minded" (James 4:8). This emphasizes the concept that approaching God requires a level of spiritual and moral purity.

For Example: Consider it like going to a formal event. You wouldn't go in your work clothes; you'd put on your best attire. Similarly, drawing near to God means "dressing" our best spiritually, striving for holiness and sincerity in our approach.

God's Reciprocal Move

The latter part of James 4:8 assures us that if we make this move, God will draw near to us. This is not a human-initiated relationship where we have to do all the work; it's a divine partnership.

Visual Aid: Imagine a bridge that connects two cliffs. You take steps on the bridge from your side, and God takes steps from His side. When both are committed to meeting in the middle, the relationship is at its best.

Real-Life Application

- **Personal Prayer:** One of the most direct ways to draw near to God is through prayer. Regular, heartfelt communication is essential in any relationship, and your relationship with God is no different.

- **Obedience:** Simply knowing what is right isn't enough. Acting upon that knowledge by living a life that pleases God is a concrete way to draw near to Him.

- **Bible Study:** The Bible is the written Word of God, and through it, we get to know Him better. This is not mere academic exercise but spiritual nourishment.

- **Fellowship:** Surrounding ourselves with like-minded believers encourages spiritual growth and enables us to draw near to God collectively.

- **Serving Others:** Sometimes we find God most when we're serving others in His name. Acts of kindness and love are not just good deeds but acts of worship that bring us closer to God.

The Ultimate Goal: Spiritual Intimacy

The principle found in James 4:8 aims at a deeper spiritual intimacy with God. Drawing near to God is an ongoing process, a spiritual journey that enriches our understanding of God and helps us become more like Him. It's like a marriage where both partners continuously learn and grow, becoming increasingly unified over time.

The Non-Negotiables

James 4:8 is also a reality check. Drawing near to God isn't a casual endeavor. There are non-negotiables involved, such as moral purity and spiritual integrity. Note that this isn't a message advocating works-based salvation but rather an explanation of the spiritual dynamics involved in a God-honoring relationship. Salvation is by faith, but a faith without works is dead, as James himself reminds us (James 2:26).

James 4:8 is more than a verse; it's a life principle. It gives us both a command and a promise. The command is to purify ourselves and to draw near to God. The promise is that if we do so, God will draw near to us. In a world full of distractions and pitfalls, this verse serves as an invaluable guide, reminding us where our focus should be—to draw nearer to God, in purity and in truth. And when we take those steps, we have the assurance that God will take His steps toward us, making our spiritual journey one that continuously moves us closer to Him.

Spiritual Practices for Intimacy with God

In the age of fast-food spirituality and quick fixes, the Christian journey may often seem like a laborious endeavor. Yet, there is a depth to knowing God that goes beyond weekly sermons or casual prayer before meals. How then can we engage with God in a manner that breeds genuine intimacy? The Scriptures give us a roadmap for deepening this most important relationship.

The Power of Prayer

"Pray without ceasing," Paul urged in 1 Thessalonians 5:17. The very idea of unceasing prayer might be intimidating, but at its core, prayer is simply conversation with God. It is talking and listening, asking and receiving. Jesus said, "Whatever you ask in prayer, you will receive, if you have faith" (Matthew 21:22).

Prayer isn't merely presenting a wish list to a divine Santa Claus. It is a practice that brings us into alignment with God's will. *Think of prayer as a phone call with a loved one that you never hang up; it remains open throughout the day, catching moments of laughter, despair, questions, and ordinary conversations.*

Delving into the Word

The Bible isn't just a historical record; it's God's revelation to humanity, a text imbued with life and meaning. "For the word of God is living and active, sharper than any two-edged sword, piercing to the division of soul and of spirit, of joints and of marrow, and discerning the thoughts and intentions of the heart" (Hebrews 4:12).

A consistent and deep study of the Scriptures provides sustenance for our spiritual lives. The Bible equips us to navigate through life's complexities and brings us closer to understanding God's character. Just like you cannot know a person deeply without spending time in conversation, you cannot know God deeply without spending time in His Word.

Fasting as a Form of Worship

While Christians are not under the Mosaic Law and are not obligated to fast, fasting can still serve as a powerful spiritual exercise when done voluntarily. It is a way of elevating the spirit over the flesh, of focusing on God rather than our earthly needs or desires. The goal is not to manipulate God into doing something for us but to align ourselves more closely with His will.

Praise and Worship

The Psalms are rife with expressions of worship and praise to God. This is not merely because Jehovah is deserving of praise, although He is, but also because worship redirects our focus from ourselves to God. It helps us to recognize His sovereignty, His goodness, and His love. *Imagine standing at the base of a mountain and looking up; you are filled with awe and your problems suddenly seem small in comparison. Worship has the same effect on our perception of life's challenges.*

Selfless Giving

Jesus taught extensively about the importance of giving, and not just in monetary terms. The Christian spirit of giving should extend to our time, our abilities, and our love. "Give, and it will be given to you. Good measure, pressed down, shaken together, running over, will be put into your lap. For with the measure you use it will be measured back to you" (Luke 6:38).

This is not a formula for getting rich but a principle that governs the Christian life. When we give selflessly, we are acting in alignment with God's character, thereby becoming more like Him.

Community and Fellowship

While personal practices are essential, the Christian life is not meant to be lived in isolation. The New Testament church was marked by a strong sense of community and mutual support. "Let us consider how to stir up one another to love and good works, not neglecting to meet together, as is the habit of some, but encouraging one another, and all the more as you see the Day drawing near" (Hebrews 10:24-25).

Intimacy with God also flows through our relationships with other believers. Through fellowship, we gain new insights into God's character, and we are often the instruments through which God chooses to answer our prayers or the prayers of others.

The Fruit of the Spirit: Evidence of Intimacy

The fruits of the Spirit—love, joy, peace, patience, kindness, goodness, faithfulness, gentleness, self-control—are the natural outgrowths of an intimate relationship with God (Galatians 5:22-23). These are not qualities we must strain to produce but are the organic results of a life deeply rooted in a relationship with the Creator.

The Rewards of Being Close to God

The notion that we can even be close to God is a staggering concept when you think about it. God, the Creator of the universe, the Source of life itself, invites us into a relationship. It's akin to a loving parent who stoops down to be on eye-level with their child. While God is almighty and infinite, He chooses to relate to us on our level, desiring closeness with us. When we reciprocate this, the rewards are manifold.

Deep Contentment and Peace

In a world that seems filled with turbulence and chaos, the serenity we get from God becomes a priceless treasure. *"Peace I leave with you; my peace I give to you. Not as the world gives do I give to you. Let not your hearts be troubled, neither let them be afraid,"* said Jesus in John 14:27. This peace isn't just the absence of conflict; it's a profound sense of well-being, knowing that you are in the care of the Almighty. Imagine being in the eye of a storm where everything is calm and still; that's the kind of peace we're talking about here—a sanctuary for the soul in the midst of life's battles.

A Clearer Moral Compass

When we are close to God, it becomes easier to discern what is right and what is wrong. The Bible guides us as a reliable moral compass, and it gets even clearer when we are close to its Author. It's similar to a student who understands a textbook far better when they have a close relationship with the professor who wrote it. We start seeing life through the lens of God's wisdom, rather than the flawed perspectives of the world.

The Joy of Purpose

Nothing can be more rewarding than knowing that your life has a purpose. When we draw close to God, we are essentially aligned with His will. Ephesians 2:10 informs us that "we are his workmanship, created in Christ Jesus for good works, which God prepared beforehand, that we should walk in them." This concept is parallel to a well-crafted tool being used for its intended purpose; the tool performs at its best and lasts longer.

Encountering Real Love

In human terms, love is often conditional, based on what one can offer or how one appears. Yet, God's love is unconditional. Romans 5:8 reveals that "God shows his love for us in that while we were still sinners, Christ died for us." This is love in its purest form, offering the ultimate sacrifice for the ultimate good of the other. Think about the safety and security a small child feels in the arms of a loving parent; this is but a dim reflection of the love we experience in closeness to God.

Spiritual Fortitude

Spiritual strength isn't about not having problems; it's about having the resilience to face them. Consider an athlete who has undergone rigorous training; when faced with a challenge, he doesn't crumble but faces it head-on. James 1:2-4 notes that "the testing of your faith produces steadfastness." In closeness to God, we find not just the strength to endure hardships but also the character to grow through them.

Divine Guidance and Wisdom

Being close to God is like having a GPS that is never wrong. In Psalm 32:8, Jehovah says, "I will instruct thee and teach thee in the way which thou shalt go: I will counsel thee with mine eye upon thee." This guidance is not a road map handed over to you to figure out on your own. It is real-time, dynamic, and takes into account all the variables that you might not even be aware of.

Eternity in Perspective

The ultimate reward is eternal life itself, either in heaven, ruling with Christ, or on a paradise Earth, as originally intended. John 3:36 warns, "Whoever believes in the Son has eternal life; whoever does not obey the Son shall not see life, but the wrath of God remains on him." Our closeness to God shapes not just our present but also our eternity.

CHAPTER 7: Steadfastness in Faith: A Lifelong Journey

The Foundation of Faith

Faith is not a one-time event but a lifelong journey. The moment we accept Jesus Christ as our personal Savior, we are ushered into this incredible spiritual voyage. This starting point is crucial; as Paul states, "For by grace you have been saved through faith. And this is not your own doing; it is the gift of God" (Ephesians 2:8). You don't build a skyscraper without laying a solid foundation, and similarly, a steadfast faith requires a strong foundation rooted in the acceptance of God's grace and Jesus Christ's sacrificial love.

The Importance of Steadfastness

Steadfastness is the act of standing firm in your faith. It isn't a passive state but an active endeavor. You must be diligent to "make your calling and election sure" as Peter wrote (2 Peter 1:10). Just like an athlete continuously trains to perform at their peak level, a Christian must remain committed to practicing their faith through regular prayer, scripture study, and obedience to God's commandments.

Trials and Testing

Life is full of trials. James doesn't say "if" you face trials but "when" (James 1:2). These trials serve as the "gymnasium" of our faith. Just as muscles are strengthened through resistance training, so too is our faith strengthened through resistance in the form of trials. It is critical to remember that God doesn't design suffering to break us, but He allows it. *Why?* It teaches humanity an object lesson about the limitations of human independence and the need for God's sovereignty.

The Role of the Bible

The Bible serves as the Christian's handbook for this journey. It's not merely a collection of ancient texts but the inspired Word of God. You don't need an indwelling of the Holy Spirit to understand it; it's the ultimate guidebook filled with practical advice and godly wisdom. The Bible encourages us, challenges us, and equips us to remain steadfast. Paul aptly noted, "All Scripture is breathed out by God and profitable for teaching, for reproof, for correction, and for training in righteousness" (2 Timothy 3:16).

Discernment and Decision Making

Free will plays a vital role in our journey. This is not a predestined path where we are mere puppets on a string. We make choices, and these choices have consequences. God has foreknowledge of our decisions, but this doesn't negate our free will. It's like a parent who knows their child so well that they can predict what choices the child will make, but that knowledge doesn't force the child's hand.

Fellowship and Accountability

No man is an island, and our faith journey isn't a solo endeavor. Being part of a Christian community provides support, encourages growth, and fosters accountability. It's like having a group of fellow travelers on a long and sometimes arduous journey. When one stumbles, the others offer a helping hand. When one strays from the path, the others provide correction. This fellowship is crucial in maintaining steadfastness.

The Eternal Perspective

Life on this earth is but a vapor, a brief moment in the grand timeline of eternity. Our eternal destiny is not universally fixed nor guaranteed by a one-time act of faith. There are no shortcuts. You can't purchase a ticket to heaven and then live your life however you please. *Eternal life is a gift offered through continued obedience and faithfulness to God.*

The Ultimate Goal

The end of our faith journey is not merely to attain salvation for ourselves but to glorify God and to bring others into a saving relationship with Him. The ultimate goal is to hear those beautiful words from our Savior, "Well done, good and faithful servant" (Matthew 25:21).

The steadfastness in faith is a lifelong journey that requires a firm foundation, active participation, and a reliance on the Bible as our guide. It involves trials and testing, exercises free will, values fellowship, keeps an eternal perspective, and aims for the ultimate goal of glorifying God. Therefore, let us be diligent in nurturing a steadfast faith, making the most of the time and opportunities God gives us, and may we all reach the end of our journey hearing the commendation from our Lord.

Understanding the Call to Steadfastness

In a world that often feels chaotic and outside our control, it's easy to lose sight of what matters. This can be especially true for Christians trying to navigate a complex society, sometimes hostile to their beliefs. At such times, steadfastness — the unwavering commitment to our convictions and faith — becomes paramount.

The Biblical Imperative for Steadfastness

The Bible is replete with exhortations for Christians to remain steadfast in their faith. In 1 Corinthians 15:58, Paul encourages believers by saying, "*Therefore, my beloved brothers, be steadfast, immovable, always abounding in the work of the Lord, knowing that in the Lord your labor is not in vain.*" He speaks not only of a static commitment but an active expression of our faith. Like a well-rooted tree that withstands all kinds of weather, a steadfast believer is resilient in the face of adversity, drawing strength from their rootedness in God's promises.

Faith as the Foundation of Steadfastness

We can liken the call to steadfastness to the construction of a building. For any structure, the foundation is the critical starting point. Our faith is that foundation. Without a strong belief system grounded in the teachings of the Bible, our resolve will crumble under the weight of challenges and trials. In Hebrews 11:1, faith is defined as "*the assurance of things hoped for, the conviction of things not seen.*" With faith as our foundation, the architecture of our Christian life can be strong and resilient, able to withstand the pressures of living in a world that often stands in opposition to godly principles.

Testing Builds Character

The concept of testing and trials is ubiquitous throughout Scripture. For instance, James writes, "*Count it all joy, my brothers, when you meet trials of various kinds, for you know that the testing of your faith produces steadfastness*" (James 1:2-3). Trials, as uncomfortable as they may be, serve a purpose.

Consider a piece of metal being forged. The metal must go through the heat and the pounding to emerge as a useful tool. Likewise, our trials test our mettle, purifying our faith and making us more like Christ. While God did not create suffering as part of His divine plan (Note 14), He allows it as a means of refining us, thereby strengthening our resolve and faith.

Steadfastness in Practice

Living a steadfast life isn't merely about believing the right things; it's about putting those beliefs into action. The Apostle John writes, "*Little children, let us not love in word or talk but in deed and in truth*" (1 John 3:18). Our steadfastness manifests in how we handle our relationships, our responsibilities, and our worship of God.

Relationships

Being steadfast in our relationships means demonstrating Christ-like love and grace even when it's difficult. Our interactions should reflect the Fruits of the Spirit outlined in Galatians 5:22-23, such as patience, kindness, and self-control.

Responsibilities

In the realm of responsibilities—whether at work, home, or church—steadfastness shows up as integrity and diligence. Colossians 3:23 instructs, "*Whatever you do, work heartily, as for the Lord and not for men.*"

Worship

Lastly, steadfastness is evident in our commitment to God's worship, not merely as a Sunday ritual but as a lifestyle. A steadfast Christian views all aspects of life through the lens of worship to God, approaching both successes and failures as opportunities to glorify Him.

The Rewards of Steadfastness

Though the path to steadfastness may be fraught with difficulties, it's not without its rewards. These rewards may not always be material or immediate, but they are promised. In 2 Timothy 4:7-8, Paul talks about the "*crown of righteousness*" awaiting those who have remained faithful.

Moreover, our steadfastness serves as a beacon for others. The more steadfast we are in our faith, the more our lives can serve as living testimonies to the transformative power of the Gospel. In a world that is often unstable and fickle, the unwavering nature of a steadfast Christian becomes a compelling argument for the truth of Christianity.

Being steadfast in faith is not a one-off act; it's a lifelong commitment. The Christian walk is less of a sprint and more of a marathon. It requires preparation, training, and most importantly, a reliance on God for strength and guidance (Note 11). Though the path may be narrow and filled with obstacles, the rewards are eternal. Our steadfastness today is a preparation for an everlasting life, an embodiment of the ultimate hope we have in Jesus Christ. So, let us "press on toward the goal for the prize of the upward call of God in Christ Jesus" (Philippians 3:14), trusting that all things are indeed working for our good.

Building Resilience in Faith

The Challenge of Faith in a Broken World

The world is often a chaotic, disheartening place. Suffering abounds, affecting both believers and non-believers. However, it's crucial to remember that while God has not designed suffering to foster growth or character, He allows it. We live in a broken world, but that does not mean God has forsaken us. When storms hit, resilience in faith becomes the linchpin that keeps our spiritual life intact.

Why Resilience is Essential in Faith

Resilience in faith isn't merely about surviving trials but thriving through them. It's about knowing that even in the face of suffering, we still have an eternal hope and a God who is in control. This type of resilience doesn't just happen; it is cultivated. When we confront suffering, God allows it not to break us but to build us. Imagine your faith like a bridge designed to withstand various weights and pressures; the stronger it is, the more it can endure.

The Role of God's Sovereignty

Understanding the sovereignty of God lays the foundation for resilience in faith. This is the bedrock belief that God is in control of all events, not as a puppet master who overrides human free will, but as a divine orchestrator who understands all potential outcomes. His foreknowledge allows Him to know all the possible routes our free will could take us. Hence, God's sovereignty never negates human responsibility. It's like a master chess player who knows every move you could make but allows you to make those moves freely.

The Importance of God's Word

Resilience in faith comes from a deep well of wisdom, and that well is the Bible. We do not have an indwelling of the Holy Spirit; instead, we're guided by the Spirit-inspired Word of God. When trials come, the Bible serves as a trustworthy guide. "Your word is a lamp to my feet and a light to my path" (Psalm 119:105). Just as a person wouldn't wander in a dark forest without a light, so we should not navigate life's trials without the illumination of Scripture.

The Commitment to Persevere

"Let us not grow weary of doing good, for in due season we will reap if we do not give up" (Galatians 6:9). Resilience involves the commitment to persevere. Perseverance is often discussed in the context of enduring hardship, but it's broader than that. It's about continuing to walk in faith, even when it would be easier not to. It's about ongoing obedience and trust in God. It's like running a marathon: you don't quit when it gets tough; you endure, knowing the reward at the end is worth the effort.

Cultivating a Resilient Community

We aren't meant to be lone wolves; we're part of a flock. The support of a spiritual community is essential for resilience. Sometimes, other people can see our strengths and weaknesses more clearly than we can see them ourselves. In times of trial, the faithful community is a net that catches us when we fall. These relationships should not be one-dimensional; just as we receive, so should we give, contributing to the resilience of the community as a whole.

God's Purposes and Our Response

While God didn't design suffering, He has a purpose for allowing it. The current state of the world serves as an object lesson for humanity, demonstrating what happens when we assert independence from God's sovereignty. When trials come, resilience in faith means trusting that God's purposes are at work, even if we don't fully understand them. It means knowing that "in all things God works for the good of those who love him, who have been called according to his purpose" (Romans 8:28).

Conclusion: Building Resilience for a Lifetime

The journey of faith is a lifelong expedition. As we move forward, let us cultivate resilience through a deeper understanding of God's sovereignty, a commitment to His Word, the will to persevere, and the support of a strong spiritual community. There will be trials, and suffering is a given in this fallen world. But when we build resilience in our faith, we can face whatever comes our way, knowing that "in all these things we are more than conquerors through him who loved us" (Romans 8:37).

The Impact of Steadfastness on Christian Walk

The Imperative of Steadfastness

Steadfastness is like a deeply-rooted tree that weathers storms and droughts alike. It remains unmoved because its roots are anchored in fertile ground. Similarly, a steadfast Christian finds their foundation in the Scriptures, holding onto their faith amid life's challenges. Steadfastness is not just a virtue; it is a spiritual necessity. Without it, we could easily be swayed by false doctrines, tempted by worldly desires, or become weary in well-doing.

Theological Foundation: What is Steadfastness?

Steadfastness is resolute adherence to a firm belief or course of action. In a Christian context, it's the unwavering commitment to the faith, anchored in a deep understanding of biblical truths. The Apostle Paul often encouraged steadfastness, like when he told the Corinthians to "be steadfast, immovable, always abounding in the work of the Lord" (1 Cor. 15:58). The steadfast Christian is not a reed shaking in the wind; they are a solid rock, unswayed by the tides of public opinion or personal trials.

Biblical Commands to Be Steadfast

The Bible underscores the importance of steadfastness in multiple places. James tells us, "Blessed is the man who remains steadfast under trial" (James 1:12). Peter also joins in, urging Christians to "resist [Satan], firm in your faith" (1 Peter 5:9). These are not mere suggestions; they are commands. The Scriptures don't give us an opt-out clause when life gets tough. Instead, we are told to remain steadfast.

Why Steadfastness is Crucial

Anchored in Truth

Being steadfast anchors us in biblical truth. It enables us to discern false teachings and protects us from spiritual pitfalls. Paul warns Timothy about those who are "always learning and never able to arrive at a knowledge of the truth" (2 Tim. 3:7). A steadfast Christian is not easily misled because they understand the fundamentals of their faith.

Resilience in Suffering

Steadfastness builds resilience. In a world that's not always friendly to Christian values, steadfastness helps us withstand external pressures. Even if the whole world turns against us, our anchor holds. Job, despite his immense suffering, displayed this type of resilience, which comes from being rooted in an unchanging God.

Preserving Our Witness

Our steadfastness also affects how others see Christianity. When people see us holding onto our faith in difficult circumstances, it speaks volumes. It becomes a living testimony that God's promises are reliable. It could well be the catalyst that encourages someone else to explore the Christian faith.

How to Cultivate Steadfastness

Study the Word

To cultivate steadfastness, one must first understand the Word. You can't stand for something you don't understand. Studying the Scriptures provides the intellectual and spiritual tools needed to remain steadfast.

Prayer and Dependence on God

Prayer is the linchpin that connects us to the source of our steadfastness—God. Through prayer, we draw strength and wisdom, which helps us remain resolute. Remember, it is God who enables us to be steadfast.

Fellowship with Believers

The Christian walk is not a solitary endeavor. We are part of a body of believers, and this fellowship helps reinforce our steadfastness. Others can encourage us, offer wisdom, and help us remain grounded. "And let us consider how to stir up one another to love and good works" (Hebrews 10:24).

Actively Serving

Steadfastness is not passive; it requires action. Serving others not only aligns us with Christ's example but also strengthens our resolve to live according to our faith.

The Eternal Impact

Steadfastness is not just for the here and now; it has eternal implications. Those who hold fast to their faith receive the promise of life everlasting. "For we have come to share in Christ, if indeed we hold our original confidence firm to the end" (Hebrews 3:14). This doesn't mean works save us, but a steadfast faith is evidence of a living, active relationship with God.

The Unyielding Power of Steadfastness

To be steadfast is to stand firm in a world that's constantly shifting. It is to be anchored in truth in a sea of relativity. It requires a commitment to integrity, even when it's not convenient; it demands resilience, even when faced with trials. Being steadfast is not just an act but a lifestyle—a deep-seated attitude that defines who we are in Christ.

When we are steadfast, we become conduits of God's grace, towers of strength in our communities, and resilient warriors in spiritual battles. We set a compelling example that can draw others to Christ. More importantly, our steadfastness brings glory to God, fulfilling our ultimate purpose in this life. Let us, therefore, strive to be steadfast, immovable, always abounding in the work of the Lord, knowing that our labor is not in vain.

CHAPTER 8: Walking Wisely in a World Governed by Satan

Understanding the Battlefield

It's important to realize that we live in a world that is not under God's direct governance but is instead ruled by Satan. The Apostle Paul refers to Satan as "the god of this world" who blinds the minds of unbelievers (2 Corinthians 4:4). This gives us a sobering context within which to understand our walk as Christians. Our life journey is a passage through enemy territory.

Distinguishing Between God's Will and Satan's Deception

Discernment is Key: We must sharpen our discernment to differentiate between God's will and Satan's deceptions. This is crucial because Satan often masquerades as "an angel of light" (2 Corinthians 11:14). Therefore, any teaching, doctrine, or practice must be scrutinized against the Holy Scriptures. This is your compass in a world filled with deceptive signposts.

The Wisdom of Spiritual Vigilance

Be Alert: Scripture reminds us to be "sober-minded" and "watchful," for "your adversary the devil prowls around like a roaring lion, seeking someone to devour" (1 Peter 5:8). In a world governed by Satan, a lackadaisical approach toward spiritual matters is a recipe for disaster. You would never stroll carelessly through a minefield; similarly, the spiritual realm demands an even greater level of alertness.

Fostering a Relationship with God

A robust relationship with God acts as our bulwark against the devil's machinations. **Frequent Prayer and Scriptural Study**: While

Christians are not under the Mosaic Law and are not obligated to fast, prayer and scriptural study are indispensable. It's not ritualistic observance but a heartfelt relationship with God that empowers us to walk wisely. Remember, we don't have an indwelling of the Holy Spirit; we are guided by the Spirit-inspired Word of God.

Making Ethical Choices

Satan often makes sin look enticing, but one must remember that "the wages of sin is death" (Romans 6:23). When we're faced with ethical dilemmas, it's not just a question of right or wrong; it's a matter of life and death, in a spiritual sense. This isn't to say that we won't be forgiven for mistakes, but habitual sinning without repentance is hazardous. No belief in "once saved, always saved" here; constant vigilance and repentance are necessary for salvation.

The Role of Suffering

While we may be quick to blame Satan for our suffering, it's critical to note that God allows suffering. This suffering serves as an object lesson, demonstrating the inherent flaw in human independence from God's sovereignty. The trials we face are not designed for our growth, but they can still serve as educational experiences, reminding us of our need for divine guidance and protection.

The Importance of Community

Christians are not lone soldiers but members of a spiritual army. Assembling together for worship and mutual encouragement is not just a pleasant social activity but a Scriptural mandate (Hebrews 10:25). As individual strands of a rope make it strong, so does the community of believers provide strength against Satan's attacks. This community is not limited by ethnicity or nationality; the Jewish people are no longer God's chosen people by virtue of birth, and God's blessings are now extended to all who accept Jesus Christ.

Eternal Prospects in a Temporal World

Finally, we must keep our eyes on the eternal prospects that God offers. This world, under Satan's rule, is fleeting and temporal. But God has promised a new heavens and a new earth where righteousness will dwell (2 Peter 3:13). Our hope is not in this world but in the world to come. Keeping this perspective makes us wise travelers through this current world, cautious yet hopeful, vigilant yet joyful.

In summary, walking wisely in a world governed by Satan demands discernment, vigilance, a strong relationship with God, ethical integrity, a proper understanding of suffering, the support of a faith community, and a focus on eternal life. By adhering to these principles, guided by the inerrant Word of God, we can navigate through Satan's world in a manner that honors Jehovah and secures our eternal future.

The Exhortation of Colossians 4:5

The Book of Colossians, penned by the Apostle Paul, serves as a rich treasure chest of doctrinal teachings and practical instructions for the believer. One such nugget of wisdom is found in Colossians 4:5, where Paul exhorts, "Walk in wisdom toward outsiders, making the best use of the time." This single verse encapsulates a profound teaching that is as relevant today as it was during Paul's time. Let's delve into the layers of meaning that can be unpacked from this verse.

Contextual Background

To understand Colossians 4:5, it is crucial to consider its context. The Colossian church was facing heretical teachings that were influencing the congregation. Paul, therefore, sets the stage by first reaffirming the preeminence of Christ and the sufficiency of His work on the cross. Then he transitions into practical instructions, one of which is our focus.

Walking in Wisdom

Defining Wisdom

The first part of Paul's statement exhorts us to "walk in wisdom." Wisdom, in the Biblical context, isn't merely about knowing what is right but also about applying that knowledge in the way we live. It is akin to building a house on a rock-solid foundation. The house here is our life, and the rock is the wisdom that comes from the teachings of Christ.

Wisdom Toward Outsiders

Paul specifies that this wisdom should be displayed "toward outsiders," meaning non-believers or those not part of the faith community. Why? It's simple; they are watching. Our behavior and actions serve as a testament to our beliefs. Like a lighthouse in a dark sea, our wisdom can guide those who are lost towards the truth of the Gospel.

Making the Best Use of Time

The Value of Time

Paul doesn't stop at wisdom. He adds another layer by telling us to "make the best use of the time." Time is a valuable resource that, once lost, can never be regained. Imagine you have a jar, and you fill it with marbles. Each marble represents a unit of your time. The jar has a limited capacity, just as our earthly lives have a limit. The way we use each marble, then, becomes a matter of eternal significance.

The Cultural Climate

Given that the Colossians were facing false teachings and cultural influences that went against the grain of Christian doctrine, "making the best use of the time" also implied that they had no time to waste on falsehoods. In today's world filled with distractions and diverging ideologies, this counsel is incredibly relevant.

The Interplay of Wisdom and Time

Paul's advice is not to just walk in wisdom or to only use time wisely, but to do both in concert. It's like cooking a complex dish. Each ingredient brings its own flavor, but it's the combination that produces the final, delightful taste. When wisdom guides our use of time, and time is maximized by applying wisdom, the result is a life that is both impactful and aligned with God's will.

The Final Takeaway

Understanding and applying Colossians 4:5 in our lives calls for an intentional approach towards living wisely, especially in our interactions with those outside the faith community. It encourages us to be stewards not only of our actions but also of our time. Doing so is not merely for our benefit; it sets a compelling stage upon which the Gospel can be displayed for the world to see.

Living according to this teaching could mean the difference between someone being exposed to the light of the Gospel or remaining in darkness. So, let us walk in wisdom and make the best use of our time, serving as beacons in a world that desperately needs the light of Christ.

Practical Wisdom for Daily Living

In this chaotic world, where it seems that the dice are always rolled against us, how do we find our footing? A lot of the answers are given to us in the very book that serves as our foundational guide to life, the Bible. This tome of ancient wisdom and divine revelation offers us a roadmap to navigate life, not only for eternal salvation but also for practical, everyday living.

The Quest for Wisdom

Wisdom is a prized possession. The book of Proverbs tells us, "Happy is the man who finds wisdom, and the man who gets understanding, for the gain from it is better than gain from silver and its profit better than gold" (Proverbs 3:13-14). Wisdom, unlike knowledge, is not just the accumulation of facts. It's about how to apply what we know in a way that is beneficial. It's akin to a master chef who not only knows the ingredients but also understands just how much of each to use, at what time, and in what combination, to create a culinary masterpiece.

How Do We Gain Wisdom?

The Fear of Jehovah is the Beginning of Wisdom. The concept of 'fearing' Jehovah (God) might sound alien to our modern ears, accustomed as we are to a version of God who is all love and no judgment. However, this "fear" is not about being scared but about having a reverential awe and respect for the Creator. "The fear of Jehovah is the beginning of wisdom; all those who practice it have a good understanding" (Psalms 111:10).

Just as a student listens attentively to a teacher or an apprentice to a master craftsman, so we should be attentive to Jehovah. Wisdom begins when we understand that Jehovah is the source of all wisdom and that we should go to Him and His Word to understand how to live.

Making Wise Choices

Making wise choices involves the ability to discern. It's like being a fruit picker who chooses the best and ripest fruit while leaving the rotten ones. The Bible offers various criteria for making wise choices. One of the most direct calls to wise decision-making is found in the book of James, "If any of you lacks wisdom, let him ask God, who gives generously to all without reproach, and it will be given him" (James 1:5).

Life is a series of choices, from the trivial to the monumental. Each choice sets a chain of events in motion. The Bible gives us the ethical and moral framework to make choices that align with God's will. It's not a list of dos and don'ts but a guide for making decisions that honor God and benefit us. It's akin to a navigational compass that always points north; the Bible always directs us toward God's will, helping us avoid the pitfalls that lead to ruin.

The Word of God as Our Guide

We are not floating adrift in a sea of relativism or uncertainty because we have the Bible as our anchor. In 2 Timothy 3:16-17, we read that "All Scripture is breathed out by God and profitable for teaching, for reproof, for correction, and for training in righteousness, that the man of God may be complete, equipped for every good work." We don't have the indwelling of the Holy Spirit, but the Spirit-inspired Word of God guides us.

Imagine you have a complex machine, and you have the manual written by the person who designed that machine. The manual has everything you need to operate it successfully. You wouldn't throw the manual away and try to figure it out yourself, would you? The Bible is that manual for life, given to us by our Creator.

Wisdom in Suffering

Suffering, often seen as a conundrum, is another area where we can apply divine wisdom. While God didn't design suffering as a character-building exercise, He allows it to occur. God allows suffering to teach humanity a critical lesson about the consequences of sin and the importance of divine sovereignty. Just like how a parent might allow their child to touch a hot stove after repeatedly warning them, God allows us to feel the ramifications of a world that has turned its back on Him, so that we may return to His protective care.

The Wisdom of Foresight and Preparation

God's wisdom is also evident in how He prepares us for life's challenges. The wisdom literature of the Old Testament is replete with verses that encourage prudent foresight and preparation. Proverbs 21:5 states, "The plans of the diligent lead surely to abundance, but everyone who is hasty comes only to poverty." Here we're reminded that planning and diligence lead to success.

Wisdom and Salvation

Wisdom doesn't just help us navigate the trials of this life; it also leads us to acknowledge the most significant truth — our need for salvation. There's no universal salvation, no 'once saved always saved', and no eternal security. Every individual has to make the personal decision to accept Christ and walk in His ways continually. We must apply wisdom in ensuring that our lives reflect this commitment to Christ.

Wisdom is not a concept to be studied but a way of life to be lived. By turning our hearts and minds toward Jehovah and His inspired Word, we set ourselves on a path that not only leads to a prosperous and fulfilling life on earth but also to eternal life. Whether we are making choices, planning for the future, or navigating through suffering, God's wisdom provides the essential framework for practical daily living. It's not just a tool for survival in this world but a critical component for thriving in God's grand design.

Living as Salt and Light in the World

The Significance of Being Salt

Jesus called His followers the "salt of the earth" (Matthew 5:13). This metaphor is rich with meaning. In ancient times, salt served many purposes; it wasn't merely a flavor enhancer as we often think of it today. Salt was a preservative that prevented the decay of food in a world where refrigeration did not exist. When Jesus called His followers salt, He was stressing their role as preservative agents in society, countering moral and spiritual decay.

Picture an old storehouse filled with meat. In such an environment, decay is inevitable unless something stops the process. That's what salt does—it stops the rot. Similarly, when Christians live out their faith authentically, their influence hinders the spread of sin and degradation. However, just as salt that has lost its taste is worthless, so are Christians who have lost their distinctiveness.

The Unmistakable Role of Light

"You are the light of the world," Jesus also said (Matthew 5:14). Light serves two primary functions: it dispels darkness and guides the way. Consider a lighthouse on a rocky shore. Its purpose is to warn ships at sea of dangerous areas and guide them safely to harbor. Christians are like that lighthouse. By living out their faith, they expose the darkness of sin and point people toward the safety of the gospel.

Imagine yourself in a room plunged into total darkness. You can't see anything. When someone lights a candle, your attention is immediately drawn to that source of light. In a similar way, a Christian's life should stand out, drawing people's attention and leading them to the ultimate source of light, which is Christ.

Preserving Truth in a Post-Truth World

We live in an age where truth is often considered relative, subjective, or even obsolete. But Jesus said, "I am the way, and the truth, and the life. No one comes to the Father except through me" (John 14:6). Christians serve as the preservers of this absolute truth. Our lives and words should validate and proclaim the eternal truths of the gospel.

It's like being a timekeeper in an age when everyone else is using broken clocks. If you keep the correct time, others can calibrate their clocks accordingly. If you falter, everyone loses the correct time. The world may not always appreciate the standard we hold, but it is essential for the spiritual and moral well-being of society.

Ethical Consistency and Social Responsibility

The apostle Paul wrote, "For you were once darkness, but now you are light in the Lord. Walk as children of light" (Ephesians 5:8). This instruction calls for a life of ethical consistency. It's easy to shine a light when you're in a room full of light. But it's when you're surrounded by darkness that your light truly makes a difference. Think of social issues like injustice, poverty, or moral decay. As Christians, we're not just to avoid these evils but to be actively involved in countering them.

Imagine you have a flashlight in a power outage. You don't just use it to navigate your own way; you also shine it so others can see and find their way. In the same vein, being salt and light isn't just for our benefit; it's for the benefit of those around us.

Caution: Do Not Lose Your Flavor or Dim Your Light

The apostle Paul cautioned, "Examine yourselves, to see whether you are in the faith. Test yourselves" (2 Corinthians 13:5). The risk exists that we can lose our "saltiness" or let our light dim. Once we compromise with the world—once we lose our distinctiveness—we lose our ability to preserve and enlighten.

Consider a flashlight whose batteries are running low. It becomes progressively dimmer until it can hardly be distinguished from the surrounding darkness. The same can happen to Christians who compromise their principles. They lose their effectiveness in a world desperately in need of moral and spiritual guidance.

Concluding Remarks

Being salt and light is not an optional aspect of Christian discipleship; it is its very essence. As salt, we are to counteract the moral decay we see in the world around us. As light, we are to dispel darkness, acting as beacons that point others to Christ. It's a high calling and a profound responsibility—one that we cannot afford to neglect.

Remember, it's not enough to merely blend in with the rest of the world. A salt particle that blends into a mound of sugar loses its distinctiveness and usefulness. A light that's covered loses its ability to illuminate. So let your light shine before others, that they may see your good works and give glory to your Father who is in heaven (Matthew 5:16). Stand firm, be vigilant, and continually seek to be what Christ has called you to be: the salt of the earth and the light of the world.

CHAPTER 9: When Things Don't Make Sense: Trusting God's Plan

The Labyrinth of Life's Challenges

Life often feels like a complex maze, filled with twists and turns that defy our understanding. You may question why you are facing trials when you have faithfully served God. Your job vanishes, a loved one falls ill, or your efforts to do good seem to bear no fruit. At such times, it's natural to ask, "Why is this happening to me?" and "Where is God in all this?"

God's Sovereignty and Human Free Will

Understanding God's role in our lives requires a nuanced view of His sovereignty and our free will. **God is not a puppet master** who controls every action and event. He allows us to make choices and, yes, even mistakes. He did not design suffering but allows it to teach humanity an object lesson about the consequences of sin and the imperfections of a fallen world.

Paul speaks of this complex relationship when he says, "And we know that for those who love God all things work together for good, for those who are called according to his purpose" (Romans 8:28). Notice that it doesn't say all things are good, but rather they "work together for good." This aligns with the idea that God knows all potential outcomes of our free will decisions and allows events to unfold in a way that fulfills His ultimate plans—without violating human freedom.

The Conundrum of Suffering

Suffering is not God's design, but He allows it. Think of it as an unfortunate side effect of human disobedience and a broken world. Yet, God can use suffering to bring about His purposes. For instance, when Joseph was sold into slavery by his brothers, it was a terrible act. But years later, Joseph could say to them, "You meant evil against me, but God meant it for good, to bring it about that many people should be kept alive" (Genesis 50:20). This exemplifies how God can use even the harsh realities of life for greater purposes.

The Role of Faith

In the book of Habakkuk, the prophet questions God about the suffering he sees. God's reply is telling, "The righteous shall live by his faith" (Habakkuk 2:4). Faith doesn't mean turning a blind eye to problems. Instead, it means trusting that God has a plan even when you can't see it.

Faith is like wearing night-vision goggles in a dark room. You might not see everything clearly, but you trust that you're not alone and that there's a way out. As the author of Hebrews wrote, "Now faith is the assurance of things hoped for, the conviction of things not seen" (Hebrews 11:1).

Awaiting God's Timing

Another aspect to consider is God's timing. You might want immediate answers or solutions, but God's timeline is not ours. King David spoke of waiting patiently for Jehovah: "I waited patiently for Jehovah; And he inclined unto me, and heard my cry" (Psalm 40:1). Sometimes, our character is shaped and refined through the trials that require us to wait.

Trusting in the Spirit-Inspired Word

We may not have the indwelling of the Holy Spirit, but we have something immensely powerful: the Spirit-inspired Word of God. This

Word equips us with the wisdom and understanding to navigate through life's complexities. "All Scripture is breathed out by God and profitable for teaching, for reproof, for correction, and for training in righteousness" (2 Timothy 3:16). Therefore, when things don't make sense, our foundation should be the unchanging Word of God.

Concluding Thoughts

When you're mired in situations that defy understanding, remember that God's ways are higher than ours. "For as the heavens are higher than the earth, so are my ways higher than your ways and my thoughts than your thoughts," says Jehovah (Isaiah 55:9). This doesn't mean we should resign ourselves to ignorance but that we should seek understanding through prayer, study, and faith.

In a world where chaos seems to be the order of the day, our anchor must be the unchanging character and promises of God as revealed in His Word. Even when we can't trace His hand, we can trust His heart. The maze of life will have its dead ends and confusing turns, but with God as our guide, we can navigate through it, confident that He is working all things for our ultimate good.

The Mystery of God's Will

Is God's Will Really a Mystery?

Many people refer to God's will as a "mystery," something incomprehensible or known only to God Himself. But is God's will truly a mystery? Or is it that our understanding of it has been clouded by misconceptions or a lack of thorough study? Let's dive deep into this subject to unravel what may seem like an enigma.

The Notion of a "Mystery"

The term "mystery" appears several times in the New Testament. For instance, Paul talks about the "mystery of God's will" in Ephesians 1:9. Here, Paul uses the term not to imply that God's will is incomprehensible, but rather to emphasize that what was once hidden has now been revealed through Christ. In essence, the "mystery" of God's will is not a question mark but an exclamation point, proclaiming God's plans and purposes clearly disclosed in the Scriptures.

"If You Do This, You Are Really My Disciples"

Jesus makes it abundantly clear that following Him comes with specific guidelines. For example, in John 8:31, Jesus states, "If you abide in my word, you are truly my disciples." Likewise, in John 13:35, He mentions that "By this all people will know that you are my disciples, if you have love for one another." Thus, Christ demystifies what is required to be His disciple: abiding in His word and love for others.

The Hundreds of "Dos" and "Don'ts" in the Bible

Throughout the Scriptures, there are hundreds of directives about what we should and shouldn't do. Some people may feel that these commands cloud the concept of God's will into a complex set of rules. However, far from making God's will a mystery, these instructions serve to clarify what God desires from us. They guide us in living a life aligned with God's principles, echoing James' counsel that "faith without works is dead" (James 2:26).

Correct Understanding Eliminates the So-Called "Mystery"

In reality, what appears as a mystery is often a result of misunderstanding or not fully grasping the text's meaning. God's will is not intended to be mysterious; it's meant to be known and lived out. For instance, God's word clearly states, "He has told you, O man, what is good; and what does Jehovah require of you but to do justice, and to love kindness, and to walk humbly with your God?" (Micah 6:8). When we align our understanding with the Biblical context and apply it properly, the so-called "mystery" unravels.

Balanced Application: The Key to Understanding

Merely understanding the words of Scripture isn't sufficient; we must apply them in a balanced manner. For example, being a good steward of God's creation doesn't mean we become activists who neglect other aspects of Christian life. Similarly, our understanding of justice and mercy should be balanced, as God is a God of both. When we overemphasize one aspect of God's will while neglecting others, that's when we can fall into the trap of perceiving it as a "mystery."

The Role of Free Will

God's sovereignty doesn't negate human free will. Foreknowledge, in this context, means that God knows all the potential paths that human free will could take. He has not predetermined our destiny; rather, He knows the outcome of every choice we could possibly make. Understanding this aspect can further demystify the concept of God's will.

The "Mystery" is for Our Discovery

God's will is not a riddle waiting to confound us but a treasure waiting to be discovered. While the Scriptures make it clear that we can never fully fathom the depths of God's mind, they also reveal enough of God's will for us to live a life pleasing to Him. Therefore, the "mystery" of God's will is not a barrier to our understanding but an invitation to dive deeper into the wisdom and knowledge of God, as revealed in the Holy Scriptures.

Biblical Figures Who Trusted God Despite Not Understanding

Abraham: Father of Nations Through Faith

Abraham had no small task ahead of him when Jehovah told him to leave his homeland and travel to a foreign land. With minimal details and without the comfort of understanding why, Abraham obeyed

God's call (Genesis 12:1-4). It's akin to being told to quit your stable job and start a business in a field you know nothing about. It doesn't make logical sense, but Abraham's trust in God did not require him to comprehend the full picture. This trust was later immensely tested when God asked Abraham to sacrifice his son, Isaac. Abraham obeyed, still not understanding why but trusting in God's greater plan (Genesis 22:1-19).

Joseph: A Story of Betrayal and Redemption

Joseph was betrayed by his own brothers, sold into slavery, and later thrown into prison on false charges. During these long years, he may not have understood why such misfortunes befell him. It's as if you're being framed at work for something you didn't do and have to serve time for it. But he continued to trust in God. Eventually, Joseph became the second-most powerful man in Egypt and saved countless lives, including those of the brothers who betrayed him. Through it all, he trusted God and even saw his hardships as part of a bigger plan: "You meant evil against me; but God meant it for good" (Genesis 50:20).

Job: The Man Who Lost Everything

Job was a man who seemingly had it all: wealth, a loving family, and good health. Yet in a short time, he lost everything. He was under no illusions that he understood why this was happening. Imagine having a great life and suddenly losing your health, wealth, and family. Despite this devastating turmoil, Job clung to his faith in God. Job could not see the cosmic contest going on behind the scenes, but he trusted God enough to say, "Though he slay me, yet will I trust in him" (Job 13:15).

Esther: For Such a Time as This

Esther became queen at a time when her people, the Jews, faced annihilation. She had to make the difficult decision to approach the king uninvited, which could have led to her death. Picture being a junior employee with critical information that could save your company, but sharing it means bypassing the hierarchy, putting your job on the line. Esther took that risk, stating, "If I perish, I perish" (Esther 4:16). She didn't understand why she was put in this precarious situation, but she trusted God and acted courageously.

Apostle Paul: Suffering for Christ

The **Apostle Paul** had a life filled with hardship and suffering after his conversion. He was imprisoned, beaten, and faced death multiple times. Yet, Paul viewed these sufferings as part of a divine strategy that he may not fully comprehend. Consider being a social activist, facing opposition, and even imprisonment for your views. You might not understand why you must endure these hardships, but you remain committed to your cause. Paul had a similar commitment to Christ. He stated, "I consider that the sufferings of this present time are not worth comparing with the glory that is to be revealed to us" (Romans 8:18).

The Power of Trust in an Unpredictable World

Life often seems like a complicated maze, filled with twists, turns, and dead ends. It's natural to yearn for a roadmap or a clear set of directions. But the reality is, God does not always provide us with understanding, and we're called to trust Him regardless. These biblical figures show us that life is not always about understanding the "why" but about trusting the "Who," which is God Himself.

The Threads of Sovereignty and Free Will

God's sovereignty and human free will intersect in a harmonious manner. While God has the power to intervene, He allows humans to make their own choices. This balance can sometimes add complexity to our life situations, making it even harder to understand why things happen the way they do. However, trusting God means accepting that He knows all the possible outcomes of our decisions and how they fit into His ultimate plan.

Embrace Trust Over Understanding

We don't always need to understand God's plan to trust Him. We often look for explanations for why things happen, but the biblical examples show us that trust is more vital than understanding. When you can't trace God's hand, you can always trust His heart. Faith in God, even when things don't make sense, opens doors to blessings and divine favor. Trusting God is a central theme in the Bible, and it is equally crucial for us today as we navigate through the challenges and triumphs of life.

Gaining Peace Through Trust

The Fundamental Importance of Trust

It's essential to recognize that trust lies at the heart of any relationship, but its utmost significance becomes evident in our relationship with God. Trusting God isn't a mere add-on to a list of spiritual attributes; rather, it serves as the foundation of our entire spiritual life. It's the cornerstone that influences how we perceive situations, people, and ultimately, how we see God Himself.

When we trust God, we declare that He is reliable, that His Word is infallible, and that His ways are not only right but also for our good. This trust manifests as peace — an inner tranquility that stands strong even amid storms. In the words of the prophet Isaiah, "You keep him in perfect peace whose mind is stayed on you, because he trusts in you" (Isaiah 26:3).

God's Sovereignty and Our Trust

The concept of God's sovereignty serves as a solid ground for our trust. Sovereignty is the idea that God is in control of everything and has ultimate authority. When we understand God's unchanging character and His unquestionable authority, it becomes easier to trust Him. He's not just a bystander; He is the one orchestrating the events of the universe.

However, this doesn't mean that God has predestined every action we take. People freely choose, and God's foreknowledge encompasses all the potentialities of these free-will decisions. God knows how they would play out in every conceivable situation. This harmonizes God's sovereignty with human free will. Trusting a God who understands every "what if" scenario brings a peace that bypasses human understanding.

Navigating Through Trials

Trust isn't something that merely blossoms in the good times; it's often refined in the fires of trials. When hardships come, and they will, trusting God becomes both a challenge and a necessity. Many wonder why God allows suffering. While it may seem that suffering is a tool for growth, it's better understood as an object lesson. God allows suffering to show the inherent flaw in human independence from His rule. In other words, suffering reveals our need to trust God even more.

Unpacking Faith and Trust

Often people conflate faith and trust, yet they are not identical. Faith is the assurance in things unseen, as per Hebrews 11:1, "Now faith is the assurance of things hoped for, the conviction of things not seen." Trust, on the other hand, is the action that flows out of this assurance. It's the feet to the faith. Faith believes God can do something, trust is living as if He already has.

Trust in Relation to Peace

Trust leads to peace because trust eliminates the need for control. We find that when we try to control every situation, peace eludes us. The peace of God which "surpasses all understanding" (Philippians 4:7) is often most evident when we are out of options and forced to rely on God. In such moments, trust generates peace because the need to control or the fear of the unknown is surrendered to God.

Why Trusting God is Beneficial for Us

It might seem counterintuitive, but trust is for our good. God doesn't need our trust; we need to trust God. When we do, our perspectives change. A problem isn't an insurmountable mountain; it's an opportunity for God to show His power. Trust doesn't make problems go away; it renders them manageable, as we realize that "we know that for those who love God all things work together for good" (Romans 8:28).

Distrust: The Thief of Peace

Distrust is not merely the absence of trust but an active form of disbelief. It's akin to a wall that not only keeps out our fears but also blocks the blessings and peace that trust could usher in. If trust brings peace, distrust brings turmoil. It's the internal war between our fears and desires, a never-ending cycle that saps our energy and leaves us anxious.

The Interconnectedness of Peace and Trust

As we see, trust isn't an isolated concept but is deeply interwoven with experiencing peace in our lives. One cannot genuinely say they have the peace of God without first establishing a firm trust in God. This trust doesn't come overnight but is a lifelong journey that grows as we continue to see God's faithfulness despite our circumstances. And in that growing trust, we find a peace that isn't dependent on external factors but is a byproduct of a relationship founded on reliance and trust in God. This isn't a theoretical peace, but a robust, life-sustaining peace that enables us to thrive in every situation because our trust is placed in the One who holds all things together.

CHAPTER 10: Final Thoughts: Never Shrink Back, Keep Walking with God

The Journey of Faith

In a world filled with trials, suffering, and moral decline, holding onto your faith can sometimes feel like holding onto a lifeline in a storm. The apostle Paul spoke to this when he said, "So we do not lose heart. Though our outer self is wasting away, our inner self is being renewed day by day" (2 Corinthians 4:16). The journey of faith is not merely a Sunday morning experience but a daily renewal of our commitment to God and His word.

Endurance as the Essential Quality

When talking about a relationship with God, endurance is often overlooked, but it's a crucial element. Jesus himself said, "But the one who endures to the end will be saved" (Matthew 24:13). Imagine running a marathon; it's not the speed with which you start that matters, but rather the consistency and the endurance to reach the finish line. Just like in a marathon, you might stumble, or even fall. However, you get up and keep going. This endurance is developed through the trials and tribulations that God allows us to go through, not because He enjoys our suffering, but as a lesson about human limitations and the need for divine guidance.

The Role of Suffering

In our human experience, suffering seems like an intruder. However, from a biblical perspective, suffering serves to underline the point that a life without God is fundamentally flawed. It's crucial to remember that God didn't design suffering to foster growth, endurance, or character but allows it to demonstrate the inherent flaw in human independence from His sovereignty. God allows suffering to teach humanity an object lesson. Job's suffering is an example that endurance and integrity can shine even in the darkest of situations when our eyes are set on God.

The Dangers of Complacency

Complacency can be a silent killer for our spiritual lives. When the Israelites became complacent, they lost their edge, and it led them down a path of sin and rebellion. King David's life is another example of how complacency can lead even the most devout believer into sin. Therefore, constantly seeking spiritual growth is essential. Hebrews 10:39 highlights the peril of spiritual complacency: "But we are not of those who shrink back and are destroyed, but of those who have faith and preserve their souls." Here the apostle Paul, the author of Hebrews, underlines the necessity to never shrink back.

The Importance of Staying in God's Word

The Bible is not merely a book of guidelines but is the inspired Word of God, offering the wisdom and knowledge we require to live lives that are pleasing to Him. Without regular interaction with the Scriptures, even the strongest believer will find it difficult to stand firm in the faith. One cannot understand the significance of Biblical truths unless one decides to embrace them, as laid out in 1 Corinthians 2:14.

Looking Forward: The Return of Christ and Final Judgment

In this era of skepticism and doubt, it's essential to remember the eschatological themes about the return of Christ and the final judgment. The apostle Peter warns us not to disregard this vital truth when he says, "The Lord is not slow to fulfill his promise as some count slowness, but is patient toward you, not wishing that any should perish, but that all should reach repentance" (2 Peter 3:9). As Christians, we have the blessed hope of Christ's return, which should serve as a catalyst for us to live holy and godly lives.

Steadfast in the Lord

It's often easier to start the journey with God than to sustain it, but it's the consistent walking with God that gets us to our spiritual destination. As Paul advises, "Therefore, my beloved brothers, be steadfast, immovable, always abounding in the work of the Lord, knowing that in the Lord your labor is not in vain" (1 Corinthians 15:58).

Never forget that our eternal fate is not predetermined, for we have the free will to choose God or to reject Him. There is no universal salvation, no once saved, always saved. Yet, the prospect before us is not one of doom but one of incredible hope and eternal life, if we remain steadfast in our faith and commitment to God. So let us keep walking with God, never shrinking back, always abounding in His work, fully persuaded that God will complete the good work He has started in us.

A Recap of the Christian Journey in Satan's World

The Starting Point: Embracing the Gospel

At the onset of our journey, we're akin to travelers navigating a maze—confused, lost, and in search of an exit. This maze is Satan's world, filled with spiritual confusion and moral chaos. It is here that we first encounter the Gospel of Christ. This Gospel is the light that pierces the darkness, showing us the way.

When we embrace the Gospel, it is like receiving a compass and a map. The Scriptures then become our ultimate guidebook, and Christ's teachings are our cardinal points. "For God so loved the world, that he gave his only Son, that whoever believes in him should not perish but have eternal life" (John 3:16). Accepting Christ is the initial, crucial step that sets the direction for the rest of our journey.

Battling Temptation and Sin

Being in Christ does not mean we won't face difficulties. We are still susceptible to sin's allure. James says, "But each person is tempted when he is lured and enticed by his own desire" (James 1:14). Imagine this as traversing through a field full of landmines. The field is the world, and the landmines are the temptations. Knowing where not to step is crucial, and that wisdom comes from God's Word.

We must constantly battle temptation, and when we fail, we have an advocate in Jesus Christ who can cleanse us from all unrighteousness (1 John 1:9). This reflects the ongoing necessity for repentance and spiritual renewal.

The Role of Suffering

The issue of suffering is akin to enduring the harsh weather conditions on our journey. We don't like it, but it's a part of the world we're traversing. While God didn't design suffering, he allows it as a way to demonstrate the inherent flaw in human independence from His sovereignty. Think of suffering as a bitter medicine that has its instructional value, teaching humanity about the importance of God's rule.

Decision Making and Free Will

Contrary to predestination, our journey is characterized by choices and free will. Our decisions are like forks in the road. God, in His foreknowledge, knows where each path will lead, but it's up to us to make the choice. Foreknowledge doesn't bind us; it simply knows us. It's a spotlight that shines on all the potential outcomes of our decisions without forcibly directing us down a predetermined path.

A Community of Believers

On this journey, we're not alone. We have a community of believers, akin to fellow travelers. Acts 2:42 describes the early Christians as devoted to "the apostles' teaching and the fellowship, to the breaking of bread and the prayers." This fellowship acts like a caravan, offering mutual support, encouragement, and collective wisdom gained from shared experiences in God's Word.

No Guaranteed Security but the Promise of Eternal Life

There is no "once saved, always saved" doctrine in our journey. Our faith must be continually nurtured and examined. Like a hiker on a perilous trail who must always be aware, we must "work out your own salvation with fear and trembling" (Philippians 2:12).

But the end of this journey offers the promise of eternal life. Contrary to the views that misconstrue Hell as eternal torment, it is a state of eternal destruction or eternal life based on one's relationship with Christ. It's the final destination, dependent on the path chosen.

The Final Destination: The Return of Christ

The ultimate goal is to be part of the Kingdom of God, which will be fully realized upon Christ's return. For those who remain faithful, the New Testament offers the hope of being part of this eternal kingdom. It's the final leg of the journey, where all things will be restored, and God's sovereignty will be fully established. It will be the end of our sojourn through Satan's world, as we are either welcomed into eternal life or face eternal destruction based on our choices and relationship with God.

Like a long-awaited dawn after a night full of hardships, the return of Christ symbolizes hope and restoration for the faithful. It aligns with eschatological themes that signify not only the end of times but also the ultimate vindication for those who have steadfastly followed Christ.

Our Christian journey in Satan's world is full of challenges, choices, and pivotal moments. Yet, it's a journey characterized by the hope and guidance that come from embracing the Gospel, making wise decisions, and living a life rooted in Christ's teachings. As we navigate through the complexities, we remain steadfast in the objective truth of

God's Word, continually encouraged by the community of believers and ultimately motivated by the hope of eternal life. This journey, tough as it may be, serves a divine purpose—it shapes us, instructs us, and prepares us for the eternal Kingdom that awaits us.

Tools for Staying the Course

In a world marred by sin, distractions, and suffering, Christians are indeed "blessed by God." Yet, we must acknowledge that we live in a realm momentarily governed by Satan (2 Corinthians 4:4). This reality demands that we employ various spiritual tools to navigate this challenging environment, especially if we aim to be recipients of God's ultimate blessing—eternal life.

The Significance of God's Word

The Bible as a Compass

The Bible is not just a collection of historical accounts, poetry, and moral teachings. It is a divinely inspired guide. In a world that continually shifts moral and ethical goalposts, the Bible remains constant. Think of it as a compass. A compass doesn't tell you where to go, but it does tell you where north is. Similarly, the Bible provides the immutable principles that help us know which direction is aligned with God's will.

Depth of Understanding

In the absence of the indwelling of the Holy Spirit, we rely solely on the written Word of God for spiritual illumination. For instance, in 1 Corinthians 2:14, the text does not imply that unbelievers cannot intellectually understand biblical teachings but that they regard them as foolishness and thus reject their import. The Word of God is our tool for deepening our understanding and for discerning how to live in a world that often promotes what is contrary to godliness.

Consistency in Prayer

A Two-Way Communication

Prayer serves as a two-way communication channel between us and Jehovah. Just like a soldier in a hostile territory maintains constant radio communication with his base, we should maintain an unbroken line of prayer with our heavenly Father. In doing so, we acknowledge our dependence on Him for wisdom, guidance, and strength (James 1:5).

Why Persistence in Prayer is Vital

Don't underestimate the power of persistent prayer. In Luke 18:1-8, Jesus told a parable about a persistent widow to show that we should always pray and not give up. If a corrupt judge could yield to the persistence of a widow, how much more will our loving Father respond to our consistent prayers?

The Role of the Christian Congregation

Strength in Numbers

The Christian congregation serves as a spiritual refuge. Here, believers assemble to engage in collective worship, mutual edification, and spiritual training (Hebrews 10:24-25). These gatherings serve as spiritual "refueling stations" where we can recalibrate our spiritual focus.

Accountability Mechanism

Additionally, fellow Christians in the congregation hold us accountable. They act as checks and balances, correcting us when we err, and encouraging us in times of weakness (Galatians 6:1-2).

Cultivating Godly Wisdom

Wisdom vs. Knowledge

While the world focuses on acquiring knowledge, the Bible places a premium on wisdom—the correct application of knowledge. It is one thing to know what is right; it is another thing to do what is right. Proverbs 2:6 tells us that Jehovah gives wisdom; from His mouth come knowledge and understanding.

Making Wise Choices

We are not predestined robots; we have the free will to make choices. However, godly wisdom helps us make choices that align with divine principles, contributing to our spiritual stability (James 3:17).

Resisting Temptation and Satanic Traps

Knowing the Enemy

It is crucial to know how Satan operates. He is not merely a concept or a symbol of evil; he is a real entity with strategies to mislead us (1 Peter 5:8). Being aware of his tactics equips us to guard against his schemes effectively.

The Armor of God

Ephesians 6:11-17 provides the metaphor of a Christian armor designed for spiritual warfare. We are to put on this full armor of God to stand against the devil's schemes. It comprises the belt of truth, the breastplate of righteousness, the shield of faith, and other elements, each serving specific defensive and offensive functions.

The Ultimate Tool: Faith

Faith as a Shield

The Bible describes faith as "the assurance of things hoped for, the conviction of things not seen" (Hebrews 11:1). It is faith that shields us from the darts of doubt, fear, and discouragement that Satan regularly launches at us.

Why Faith is Non-Negotiable

Faith is the indispensable tool in our spiritual toolbox because without it, it's impossible to please God (Hebrews 11:6). It is the bedrock on which all other spiritual tools rest. For instance, prayer without faith is merely words thrown into the wind. Similarly, reading the Bible without faith turns it into mere literature rather than the living and active Word of God (Hebrews 4:12).

Living as a Christian in a world governed by Satan requires vigilance, strategic planning, and the consistent use of various spiritual tools. These tools—the Bible, prayer, the Christian congregation, godly wisdom, awareness of satanic tactics, and above all, faith—equip us to navigate this world successfully. By employing these tools effectively, we can live lives that are not just blessed temporarily but eternally.

The Hope and Promise of Eternal Life

The Glimmering Light of Hope

In a world filled with suffering, loss, and uncertainty, the concept of "eternal life" is like a beacon of hope, a glimmering light at the end of a dark tunnel. For Christians, this isn't a vague, unsubstantiated hope, but a solid promise, fortified by the very words of Scripture. Let's delve into what the Bible reveals about this magnificent promise.

Biblical Foundation: Where It All Begins

The hope for eternal life isn't a New Testament innovation; it has roots deep within Old Testament scriptures. The prophet Daniel foretold, "And many of those who sleep in the dust of the earth shall awake, some to everlasting life, and some to shame and everlasting contempt" (Daniel 12:2). The concept was always there, like a seed waiting for the right time to sprout.

The Arrival of Christ: The Hope Manifested

With the advent of Jesus Christ, the hope of eternal life shifted from a concealed seed to a blooming flower. Jesus frequently spoke about eternal life, assuring His followers that they would have it through faith in Him. "For God so loved the world, that he gave his only Son, that whoever believes in him should not perish but have eternal life" (John 3:16). Imagine this as a long-awaited harvest, where the fruits of eternal life are finally available to be plucked.

The Crucial Role of Resurrection

One might wonder, what's the big deal with resurrection? Why is it pivotal for eternal life? Simply put, resurrection is the gateway to eternal life. The apostle Paul wrote, "But if there is no resurrection of the dead, then not even Christ has been raised. And if Christ has not been raised, your faith is futile; you are still in your sins. Then those also who have fallen asleep in Christ have perished" (1 Corinthians 15:13-18). Without resurrection, eternal life is an empty promise, like an unopened gift that can never be enjoyed.

Eternal Life Is Not Universal: The Terms and Conditions

Contrary to popular misconceptions, eternal life is not universally guaranteed. The Bible is clear: "Whoever believes in him is not condemned, but whoever does not believe is condemned already, because he has not believed in the name of the only Son of God" (John 3:18). This means that faith in Christ is not an optional add-on but a vital prerequisite for inheriting eternal life. No faith, no life—it's as straightforward as that.

Quality Over Quantity: What Kind of Life Awaits?

When we talk about eternal life, it's not merely about living forever. It's about the quality of life. Jesus said, "The thief comes only to steal and kill and destroy. I came that they may have life and have it abundantly" (John 10:10). The Greek word for "abundantly" suggests something that goes beyond mere existence, something rich and satisfying. Imagine living in a land where love, peace, joy, and righteousness reign supreme. This is the essence of eternal life.

The Final Destination: Heaven or Earth?

Another important question is, where will this eternal life be lived? According to the Bible, there are two ultimate hopes for humanity. One is to live eternally in heaven, ruling with Christ. The other is to live on a renewed earth, replete with the perfection originally intended by God. Both destinies are magnificent, each with its unique glory and beauty.

Eternal Life Is a Present Reality: Already but Not Yet

Here's where it gets more fascinating: for those in Christ, eternal life is not just a future hope but also a present reality. Jesus said, "Truly, truly, I say to you, whoever hears my word and believes him who sent me has eternal life. He does not come into judgment, but has passed from death to life" (John 5:24). This creates a paradoxical situation where eternal life has "already" begun for believers but "not yet" reached its fullness.

The Irrevocable Promise

In summary, eternal life is a rock-solid promise given by God to those who put their faith in Jesus Christ. The hope for it has deep roots in the Old Testament, which blossomed into a beautiful reality with the coming of Jesus. Eternal life is not universal but granted to those who meet the terms and conditions laid down in Scripture. It promises not just unending existence but a quality of life beyond our wildest dreams. And for those in Christ, this beautiful life has already begun, even if its fullness awaits the future.

We live in a world that's often marked by tragedy and sorrow. But for the Christian, these temporal sufferings are not the final word. Instead, they serve as stepping stones leading to an eternal life that will outshine all darkness and eclipse all despair. It's this irrevocable promise that enables us to live with hope, resilience, and unshakable faith, even in a world that often seems dominated by the contrary.

Edward D. Andrews

www.ingramcontent.com/pod-product-compliance
Lightning Source LLC
Chambersburg PA
CBHW070449050426
42451CB00015B/3408